Praise for *Right Her[e]*

'We often hear that women can play a critical role in the global response to climate change, but we seldom go beyond that statement. Natalie shows us the still unused potential we have as women and how to live climate responsibility in our daily lives.'

Christiana Figueres, former Executive Secretary of the UN Framework Convention on Climate Change

'What beautiful storytelling straight from the heart. This is a rallying call to women everywhere to be part of the solution for the climate crisis. Natalie helps us not just to imagine the transformational changes we need in this critical decade for action, but to get going right now in our own lives.'

Mary Robinson, former President of Ireland and UN High Commissioner for Human Rights

'*Right Here Right Now* is all about individuals getting engaged in the fight against climate change. Natalie Isaacs exemplifies that very message in her own life and in this book. Each of us, especially women, are the change agents the climate movement needs right here right now. Our voices and our actions are critical. Let's join the fight!'

Hilda Heine, former President of the Marshall Islands

'If you feel overwhelmed thinking of the climate crisis and what it means for our kids then stop right here. You are not alone and together – one meal, one conversation, one energy bill, one flood or fire response, one harvest, one vote at a time – we can change the track we are on. We can gather speed and momentum. We can ensure we won't leave people behind. We can support and inspire each other. This book is sustenance for the work we have to do ahead of us. It is hope.'

Rachel Kyte, former Special Representative of the UN Secretary-General for Sustainable Energy for All

Natalie Isaacs is the founder and CEO of 1 Million Women, a global movement of women and girls who fight climate change by changing the way they live and the way they use their economic power, their influence and their vote.

A former cosmetics manufacturer, Natalie realised that individual and collective action is a powerful path to solving the climate crisis. She decided to leave behind the overpackaged world of skin and beauty care to create an organisation that inspires and empowers women to act.

Under Natalie's leadership, 1 Million Women has grown from scratch into a movement of more than 1,000,000 women. A sought-after presenter and the *Australian Geographic* society's 2017 Conservationist of Year, Natalie delivers a simple message that resonates with women and girls of all ages, the story of her journey from apathy to climate action cutting through complexity. She is a pioneer in the gender and climate change arena in Australia, and is recognised and supported by some of the world's most influential women climate leaders.

RIGHT HERE RIGHT NW

NATALIE ISAACS

ABC
BOOKS

The ABC 'Wave' device is a trademark of the
Australian Broadcasting Corporation and is used
under licence by HarperCollins*Publishers* Australia.

HarperCollins*Publishers*
Australia • Brazil • Canada • France • Germany • Holland • India
Italy • Japan • Mexico • New Zealand • Poland • Spain • Sweden
Switzerland • United Kingdom • United States of America

HarperCollins acknowledges the Traditional Custodians
of the land upon which we live and work, and pays respect
to Elders past and present.

First published in Australia in 2022
by HarperCollins*Publishers* Australia Pty Limited
Gadigal Country
Level 13, 201 Elizabeth Street, Sydney NSW 2000
ABN 36 009 913 517
harpercollins.com.au

A catalogue record for this book is available from the National Library of Australia

ISBN 978 0 7333 4229 5 (paperback)
ISBN 978 1 4607 1461 4 (ebook)

Cover design by Mietta Yans, HarperCollins Design Studio
Cover image by shutterstock.com
Author photograph by Jenny Khan
Typeset in Arno Pro by Kirby Jones

Printed and bound in the UK using 100% Renewable Electricity at CPI Group (UK) Ltd

Harper, Elijah and Noa – my grandchildren.
Every moment of every single day I do what I do for you. Every bit of CO_2 that I can prevent from entering the atmosphere, every person I can influence to do the same, every mind I can change, every voice I can help empower, every community I can engage is for you, and for all the generations to come.

CONTENTS

Chapter 1: My Climate Journey   1

Chapter 2: Our Critical Decade   23

Chapter 3: Optimism as a Strategy   41

Chapter 4: Women's Truth to Power   59

Chapter 5: Young Women Rising   85

Chapter 6: Become the Storyteller   97

Chapter 7: Connect with Country   111

Chapter 8: A Farewell to Consumerism   133

Chapter 9: The Spirit of Community   159

Chapter 10: New Dawn for Politics   175

Chapter 11: The Day-to-Day Stuff   189

Chapter 12: A New World   219

Chapter 13: Circle of Women   233

Postscript   247

A Special Gift from Aunty Bea and her Circle   252

Endnotes   261

Resources   266

My Thanks   276

1

MY CLIMATE JOURNEY

We all share a climate. We share its past, and we share in shaping its future. Right now we are at a critical moment for the Earth's climate, which means we share responsibility for what we can do about it today.

Taking action on things I can directly influence has been fundamental to my evolution since the earliest days in my own climate journey. Getting my electricity bill down, reducing my food waste, buying less stuff, saying no to overpackaging – these things were all within my immediate control. Achieving an action, however big or small, propelled me on to the next step, because I was seeing results, and wanted to do more.

The upside was clear. I had more money in my pocket. I had come away from the shopping centre with only what I needed. I was seeing less going into my bin. I was actually feeling as though I'd been set free, thanks to my new less-is-more kind of life. When I saw these immediate results, I began to see the connection between the way I lived and the planet that I live on.

I realised everything I did *was* connected to Earth. I felt this in my heart, not just logically in my head. Making that emotional connection was profound.

To this day, I will tell anyone who'll listen to just get going – to act in your own life, no matter how small the action you start with. That action leads to more action, which will lead to big lifestyle change, which leads to feeling powerful because you really are empowered. You find your confidence, and your voice and your storytelling, and suddenly you're on track to transform your entire life, and to confidently demand more from governments, big brands and corporations.

The moment everything changed

My own breakthrough came in 2006. It was a hot, fiery early spring, which seemed to underscore the message of the film I was watching. It was US Vice President Al Gore's breakthrough documentary, *An Inconvenient Truth*. The Academy Award-winning film laid bare the climate challenge for humanity. It offered a new narrative that stripped away the overwhelming complexity of climate change, and it began to map out a set of actions we could all take.

Until then, I'd been living my life as a disengaged citizen of Earth, strangely detached from any consequences of my actions or lifestyle. Suddenly, along with many others, I sat up and started to understand both how serious the challenge of climate change was and how I could engage with the climate crisis as an individual and as part of a collective.

In these early years, I saw things quite simplistically. Burning coal to create steam to spin turbines to generate the electricity to power my home was a big greenhouse gas pollution problem, and a primary cause of the human-induced global warming. So I responded directly, in my daily life, by working on cutting my family's household electricity use in order to reduce our contribution to climate change.

I started switching more things off, to eliminate waste. I studied our electricity usage and found ways to trim it. I ditched our clothes dryer, using sun and wind and the backyard clothesline instead, and swapped out our old-style incandescent light globes, replacing them with energy-efficient compact fluorescent lights. Pretty soon I'd cut our electricity use by one-fifth, and our energy bill went down too.

Excited and encouraged, I looked for other opportunities around the house. I discovered that food waste was an enormous contributor to the climate crisis, and I led my household to cut our food waste too. We took more care buying food and stored it better, paid more attention to 'use by' and 'best before' dates, did more with leftovers, sent less to landfill and became more conscious as consumers.

For me, these small actions led to the birth of a right here right now agenda, one in which you see results that bring about immediate positive change – however big or small – and then move on to another thing, and then another. The more I did, the more empowered I felt, and the more I wanted to do.

The more I did, the more empowered I felt, and the more I wanted to do.

My family's negative impact on the planet, our footprint, was being reduced. But at the same time, our quality of life was as good as ever – we were saving money by consuming less, and we felt better about our impact on the planet.

Before this personal awakening, I'd felt powerless about climate change; it felt too immense and overwhelming, so why should I even try ...? Once I saw the results from making changes in my daily life, though, and realised I was preventing heat-trapping greenhouse gas pollution from going into the atmosphere, I began to understand that I was a powerful player in the story.

In that moment of personal action, when I realised my power, I knew I needed to do all I could to leave the world a better place for my children, and now my grandchildren, too, and all the generations who will follow.

And if individuals, in our millions and billions, were doing what I had just done – taking practical actions in our own daily lives to cut waste and greenhouse gas pollution – that must add up, right? It must add up as a powerful force: not only to prevent greenhouse gas pollution, but also to shift governments, big business, and human society as a whole.

I was hooked. I had found my confidence. I wanted to know more, do more. I had changed my life, and that in itself was an unstoppable force. And I wanted to share my experience so I could help other women, those who had felt the way I had – disengaged from the rising emergency of climate change – empower themselves to change their own lives too.

1 Million Women begins

Out of this grew 1 Million Women, launched in 2009 with a mission to engage literally a million women to reduce their footprints across their whole lifestyle – home, work, food, fashion, shopping, travel.

In those early days of 1 Million Women, we were teaching women and girls about living climate action in all aspects of our lives. And we are still doing this, over a decade later, because it's as important as ever. We were raising awareness about climate change and also educating people about the impact of human activities on global warming.

We pointed out that the climate crisis is a human-made problem, which began with the birth of the Industrial Revolution in the mid-18th century, and the dramatic rise in the use of fossil fuels that followed. By digging up coal to power their machines, and subsequently oil and gas, the early modern industrialists were simultaneously reinventing economic development and sowing the seeds of a huge new challenge for humanity.

We were explaining the core role that burning fossil fuels plays in the climate story, taking carbon from its safe natural storage in the ground and seabeds and turning it into pollution and exhaust. How these increased levels of carbon dioxide and other greenhouse gases like methane were then accumulating in the atmosphere, where they form a blanket around the Earth, preventing excess heat from being radiated back into space.

We used to debate whether to call it 'global warming' and 'climate change', which sounded too mild given what was at stake, or whether we needed to elevate our language and urgency to terms like 'global heating' and 'climate crisis'. Today there's absolutely no question the world is heating up rapidly, heading into a temperature danger zone. We know we are facing a crisis for the planet's climate, and in terms of time to act, it's now an emergency.

From the beginning, we implicitly recognised women often experience climate problems, and solutions, differently from men. We were seeing market research showing that, on average, women were more concerned for the wellbeing of the environment and future generations than men. We also saw that women were doing most of the day-to-day purchasing that drives household consumption. At the same time, we knew that women were overwhelmingly underrepresented in climate-related debates and decision-making, and around the negotiating table on climate – and in governments and corporate boardrooms where big decisions were being made.

Women were (and still are) 51 per cent of the population, but our voices weren't being heard, or were being disregarded. Too few people were really thinking about a gender dimension for climate awareness and action. This mirrored the broader, chronic underrepresentation of women in positions of power, a gender equity deficiency which women are still struggling to overcome.

I began to truly understand that climate change is not equal, and that its consequences do not fall equally around the world. People living in developing nations, who have contributed the *least* to the climate crisis, are the ones with the *most* to lose. And it's the women and children of these countries who are already the most vulnerable: four out of five people being displaced by climate-related disasters around the world are women and girls.[1]

Even within the richest countries in the world, inequality persists. In Australia, where I live, First Nations people are disproportionately affected by climate change, and so are other low-income, disadvantaged and marginalised groups. When your planet is overheating, simply not being able to afford air-cooling is a climate-driven disadvantage.

I am a privileged white woman who has never suffered having to live in a place with noise pollution, lack of recycling facilities, zoning inequities or unreliable electricity. I've lived for decades in a suburb with green open spaces and easy access to the beach, with a cooling coastal sea breeze in all but the hottest weather. I can dive into the ocean any time I want to cool off from a sweltering hot day.

Yet an hour's drive to the west of me is Penrith, in Sydney's sprawling western suburbs, which on 4 January 2020 reached a temperature of 48.9°C, making it the hottest place on Earth that day. So what about the people who don't have access to a cooling ocean, on a nearly 50°C day, with little shade and air cooling sending power bills sky-high?

This is the lived experience of many. In late 2018, 1 Million Women surveyed 5000 women across Australia, asking them a dozen questions on what they were thinking about in regard to climate change. A strong majority (87 per cent) told us that they were experiencing discomfort from heatwaves and rising temperatures.

It's clear that a lot needs to change. Women can lead the way, working to drive climate action however and wherever we can. We can support each other. And we need to support those who are most vulnerable, stand up for them and help make their lives better and safer. Women everywhere have so much to offer to put the world on a better path, and even the smallest of actions makes a difference.

We need to support those who are most vulnerable, stand up for them and help make their lives better and safer.

Coming of age

This came home to me in full in May 2019, when 1 Million Women celebrated its 10th anniversary. We marked the occasion with our inaugural LoveEarth Festival, attended by more than 2500 guests. This joyous event, held at Sydney's leading sustainable entertainment venue, Carriageworks, was a genuine celebration of climate action, and we really did party.

Australian music legends Midnight Oil played a special gig for us, and the Prime Minister of New Zealand, Jacinda Ardern, sent us a big message of support. Australian artists Montaigné, Katie Noonan, Heidi Lenffer and the AIM Choir belted out our 1 Million Women anthem, 'You're the Voice', and the magical Emily Wurramara, First Nations songbird, opened the show with her iconic song 'Black Smoke'.

This beautiful event signalled our coming of age. We had really become a global movement of over a million women! We were celebrating all of our work and dedication, and our shared understanding that how we live each day is critical to solving the climate crisis. And we showcased clean technologies, like electric vehicles and smart energy-monitoring devices, and sustainability brands and programs helping us all to live more lightly on the planet.

Our LoveEarth Festival reflected an emerging theme for us: we have to learn, each and every one of us, how to truly love the Earth, which sustains people and all of the wonderful lifeforms and amazing places we know, as well as cutting carbon out of lives. Suddenly we had two big themes: practical action multiplied by millions of women, and loving the Earth, wherever we are and whatever we do.

Unfortunately, our 10th anniversary year ended in climate disaster. In December 2019, my family and I found ourselves, as holiday travellers, caught up in the terrible Black Summer bushfires. These fires ravaged Australia for months as the grand finale of a prolonged drought made all the worse by record heatwaves linked directly to human-induced global heating.

It's horribly simple. The hotter it gets, the drier the droughts, and the more frequent and intense the fires.[2] The language of climate now includes terms like 'megastorms', 'megadroughts', and 'megafires', and the highest bushfire danger rating in Australia is 'catastrophic' or 'code red'.

Many people suffered far worse than my family's experience of being evacuated from the iconic Snowy Mountains National Park on New Year's Eve, 2019. Though we got off lightly, we still felt the fear as skies above us turned ugly and fiery on a truly apocalyptic day. Elsewhere, close by, people were losing their homes, their livestock and, in some cases, their lives.

Over months of fires, scientists estimate some 24 million hectares were burned out. Three billion native animals were killed or displaced, and rare and endangered ecosystems were ravaged.[3]

Around the world, similarly devastating climate-related natural disasters have been unfolding in many places: fires, floods, drought-driven famines, and 'megastorms'. It's exactly what scientists and their climate modelling have been warning us about for decades, only now the emergency is real, and the evidence is all around us. Mother Earth is telling us we have to act, at unprecedented scale and urgency, yet nowhere near enough of us have been listening.

While fires were still raging in my part of the world, the COVID-19 pandemic took hold, plunging the world into a new global crisis. The 1 Million Women team had been planning a second LoveEarth Festival to follow our 10th anniversary bash, but suddenly our world had changed and everyone was scrambling to adjust. Big gatherings were off, at least in a physical sense. Cue Zoom. The pandemic became a here-and-now existential threat for humanity, which overlaid our greatest existential threat of all, the ever-present climate crisis.

I quickly came to see COVID-19 and the climate crisis as being interwoven, not just in terms of cause and effect, but in what they could tell us about our world, about ourselves, and about what was needed to ensure greater fairness and equality. As with the climate crisis, the impacts of the pandemic fell hardest on the poorest and most marginalised peoples around the world. And as with the climate crisis, there is no global solution to the pandemic unless we solve it for everyone.

More than two years on, COVID-19 has continued to surge globally. The whole world feels weary from ceaselessly fighting an invisible, shapeshifting foe. For me, this speaks loudly to our climate challenge too, because addressing the climate crisis has been playing out over decades. Maintaining stamina and personal morale, keeping our heads in the game and being mentally and physically resilient are all part of the equation.

For several years, from the end of 2009 onwards, Australia and the world experienced a deep and deeply misguided backlash against climate science and warnings. The politics and public debate around climate became increasingly toxic, destroying much of the progress from the previous decade. We lost so much time before public alarm and demand for action began to swell again in recent years, when scientific modelling and predictions have been reinforced by terrible lived experience around the world.

That lost time makes solving this crisis harder than ever. In the 2020s, we're on a precipice, with no margin for any more delay or procrastination.

So here I am in the early months of 2022, putting the finishing touches to the manuscript for this book. It's my second, following *Every Woman's Guide to Saving the Planet*, first published by ABC Books/HarperCollins in 2018 in Australia, and then internationally, including in the United Kingdom and the United States.

My journey, and 1 Million Women's, has shifted again, responding to the times in which we live. Because this is the critical decade for climate action and we must respond as never before – each and every one of us. To stave off disaster we will all have to make significant changes to our lifestyles, economies and methods of powering our industries, homes and transport, and we need to do this at unprecedented speed and scale before the decade's end.

The year 2030 does not seem far away, and we've all seen in recent years how swiftly the world can change. We are already in the decade that counts, and we need sweeping change from across society, and heartfelt optimism and absolute determination, to see us through.

The world needs to keep average global heating from human-induced climate change to below 1.5°C, lest we risk an irreversible slide into catastrophic impacts from runaway climate change.

The science is absolutely clear: if we continue burning fossil fuels at current rates, the Earth will keep on getting hotter. We'll go straight through 1.5°C of average global temperature rise, and then we'll keep going higher. According to the World Meteorological Organization,[4] the warmest seven years on record have all been in consecutive years since 2015, the same year the goal of limiting average global heating to 1.5°C was agreed on by 192 nations under the United Nation's historic Paris Agreement.[5]

In January 2021, United Nations Secretary-General António Guterres warned:

Today, we are at 1.2 degrees of warming and already witnessing unprecedented weather extremes in every

The year 2030 does not seem far away, and we've all seen in recent years how swiftly the world can change.

region and on every continent. We are headed for a catastrophic temperature rise of 3 to 5 degrees Celsius this century. Making peace with nature is the defining task of the 21st century. It must be the top priority for everyone, everywhere.[6]

My friend and mentor Mary Robinson stressed the urgency of the years ahead to 2030 when I spoke to her for this book. Without diminishing how serious the consequences of climate change could be, she also highlighted the here-and-now opportunity to make our world better by rising to the climate challenge.

Mary came to international influence as the first woman to become President of Ireland, and later was a United Nations Special Envoy on Climate Change. A lawyer by profession, she remains a tireless campaigner for climate justice, and equity between the richest nations and those struggling to catch up, especially in Africa.

In the early days of 1 Million Women, when we were just starting to make our way on the global scene, Mary noticed us. Her support started with publicly mentioning 1 Million Women as an example of women taking charge and acting in their own lives. Mary was a keynote voice at our first big event at Sydney Town Hall, and at many other events since, and she devoted an entire chapter to me and 1 Million Women in her own book called *Climate Justice: Hope, Resilience and the Fight for a Sustainable Future* (2018).

For this book, I asked her about her sense of urgency for this decade, and I also tapped into her global view spanning the developed and developing worlds.

2030 is only nine years away, [she said]. And why do we not talk more about how exciting it's going to be when we have achieved what we need to achieve? Because we will already see that the air will be cleaner and much healthier.

Over five million people die every year from indoor and outdoor air pollution. The indoor is the cooking (on traditional cookstoves burning charcoal, wood, and other combustibles like dry cattle dung). If we can get clean cooking to women in Africa, which is one of the [UN Sustainable Development Goals] objectives before 2030, then that will have a huge impact on their lives, on their livelihoods, on their time. And women will be able to do so much more because they won't be going further for firewood and depleting forests.

Mary's example shows with wonderful clarity just how closely women's economic and domestic liberation is entwined with a better climate future. And her vision is sweeping.

We're going to see the greening of cities, and the regeneration of areas, and a whole emphasis on how small farmers can conserve. We're going to see homes much more efficient, so people will use less electricity. We won't have the food waste we have now, and we'll have a circular economy; not just the recycling we're doing at the moment, but actually getting to the stage where we're reusing things.

We can all consume less and throw away less, and make it clear to producers that there's no good in producing all of this *stuff*. All of these are issues that are going to make our lives better. And in nine years' time, we should have taken a big step towards that.

So 2030 has become our line in the sand. Our old system is broken, and this is our opportunity to create a new one that is better. We all have to plant a foot, take a stand, and then step onto the path to transforming our world and our own lives.

Our old system is broken, and this is our opportunity to create a new one that is better.

We have a here-and-now opportunity to reset our world in this decade.

In the past decade, clean energy from the sun and the wind has become a global force for economic and environmental transformation, putting the end of coal and a switch to 100 per cent renewables in sight. The International Energy Agency's *World Energy Outlook* report, published in 2021,[7] says a 'low emissions revolution' is long overdue, and that the energy sector needs to be 'at the heart of the solution to climate change'.

Half of all cars being purchased by 2030 will need to be 100 per cent electric, to push the fuel-burning internal combustion engine towards its own extinction. Governments and corporations will need to have reduced their carbon pollution emissions by at least half. We all need to reduce our own footprints by half as well – and we can start right here, right now.

This critical decade is simultaneously a time for alarm and a time for great hope. We have to act like our own lives and the futures of everyone we love depend on it – because that's the truth. And it's what this book is about.

Creating the future together

This book is my outpouring of the knowledge and understanding I've gained over the 12 years I've been acting on climate change. My journey into our climate reality has been a transformative personal experience. It's been the greatest awakening of my life.

Through creating 1 Million Women, I've been privileged to gain an inside view into crucial public and private forums where the future of our world is being debated and influenced. I've travelled to the annual United Nations climate summits in Warsaw, Lima, Paris, Marrakech and, most recently, Glasgow.

Everywhere I go I meet women who are on their own climate journeys whatever that level may be. Women leading with solutions. Women leading their communities. Women who were disengaged like I was, moving from the camp of inaction into completely transforming their lives and finding their voices.

Right Here Right Now is my rallying call to women. It carries the voices of amazing women I've met and learned from: local community leaders and international leaders, First Nations Elders and scientists, and activist campaigners and policymakers like Mary Robinson, all working to change how we relate to each other, and to our one and only planet.

We need to work together to create transformative change in this crucial decade. While so much work has been done already, and is still being done, by so many incredible women, the truth is we need more women leading on climate in every facet of society.

We need more women at the table at the highest level of climate negotiations, in politics and in corporate boardrooms, and we need more women guiding our communities and families and friends. Change can happen at every level, within every role we play in our lives.

This decade needs us. We need each other. And so I hope my book changes the way you think and act. If I can persuade you to think differently about how you live on this planet in this decade, and show you how you can use your agency to drive action and shift others, then this book is doing its job.

2

OUR CRITICAL DECADE

We are in an emergency. With just one planet to call home, our right here right now mission is all about what we can do to rein in global heating in less than a decade: by 2030. To wait any longer is reckless with so much at stake. As citizens of Earth, we can't wait for governments and big vested interests in industry and commerce to move at their pace. We can forge ahead, and force the pace.

To develop our action plan for this decade of transformation, we first need to confront what climate science is telling us. It can feel overwhelming, but being informed is the first step towards creating a strong foundation from which to act and to build our resilience.

The world's leading climate scientists have spelled it out for us – both the threats, and our human complicity in creating them – in the 2021 report from the Intergovernmental Panel on Climate Change (IPCC), which has been widely interpreted as a code red for humanity.

Luckily, 1 Million Women has Professor Lesley Hughes as our climate change adviser. Lesley has worked on earlier IPCC reports as a lead author and is a Distinguished Professor of Biology and Interim Executive Dean of Science and Engineering at Macquarie University in Sydney, as well as a founding Councillor of the Climate Council of Australia.

Lesley's own scientific research focuses mainly on the impacts of climate change on species and ecosystems, and she brings a deep understanding of what's happening to our natural world and its implications for all humanity. Her reading and analysis of the latest IPCC report, and related scientific work, helps us to understand what we face.

It's scary. This is how the IPCC sees it circa 2021, translated for us by Professor Hughes:

Climate change is widespread, rapid and intensifying. It's unequivocally linked to human activities. Far from hitting peak pollution and then turning things around, we're still on track for a 1.9°C–2.4°C rise in global temperatures by the mid-21st century, and 2.7°C–3°C by the year 2100. We're likely to exceed 1.5°C in the early 2030s, with between 0.2°C and 0.6°C of further average temperature rise already 'locked in' because of our emissions over the past few decades.

To put these figures in context, they affect much more than the average daily temperature. It's hard to imagine that it would matter very much if you were headed out to the beach on a hot summer's day and I told you it was going to be 1.5°C hotter than previously expected. Who can really tell the difference between 30°C and 31.5°C?

But when we are talking about averages and the heat-driven planetary engine of the Earth's climate, it's a big deal. For example, scientists say a 1.5°C rise means the Arctic being ice-free in summer once in every 100 years; but 2°C would mean once in every 10 years. Even that seemingly small shift in temperature means that once-a-century weather events will effectively occur every decade.

The Commonwealth Scientific and Industrial Research Organisation (CSIRO), Australia's lead scientific research body, contributes to the IPCC reporting, and has gone behind the scenes on the 1.5°C question in an official blog post. What the CSIRO says makes it abundantly clear how important even small temperature variations can be, while still offering hope that we can limit the average temperature rise to 1.5°C.

It's still possible for Earth to keep below 1.5°C global warming this century, if we rapidly cut emissions to net-zero [which means any ongoing pollution being balanced out by emission savings and renewables elsewhere] ... However, if maintaining 1.5°C is not possible, the next goal should be to limit global warming to 1.6°C, then 1.7°C and so on. Limiting warming to the lowest possible level is the most important goal. Every bit of warming we avoid will reduce the climate risks we face.[8]

As Professor Lesley Hughes' review tells us, the concentration of carbon dioxide, the main greenhouse gas in the atmosphere, is up nearly 50 per cent since pre-industrial times, and now sits at the highest level in at least two million years.

The concentration of carbon dioxide, the main greenhouse gas in the atmosphere, is up nearly 50 per cent since pre-industrial times.

Carbon dioxide is not the only greenhouse gas on the rise in the atmosphere because of human activity. Methane comes from many sources, ranging from prolific cow burps, to thawing permafrost, to the so-called 'natural gas' we use in our homes and industries, and the 'landfill gas' that forms in our rubbish tips when we throw away organic waste and leave it to rot anaerobically.

Once in the atmosphere, a molecule of methane traps much more heat than a molecule of carbon dioxide, although it's not as long-lasting. There's now more methane in the atmosphere than at any time in the past 800,000 years, which also means any time since our human species evolved about 200,000 years ago. And it's up by more than 150 per cent since 1750, shortly before the Industrial Revolution kicked off.

Lesley cites a recent NASA report that shows we've already hit 1.2°C of warming above pre-industrial levels. Oceans are already 30 per cent more acidic, on average, than in pre-industrial times, because carbon dioxide in the atmosphere is being absorbed by the sea water, creating carbonic acid that in turn adversely affects development of key marine species, especially shellfish, because it reduces their ability to make their shells. Sea level rise related to global heating has accelerated to three times the level observed in the 1990s.

Already catastrophic changes, known as 'tipping points', cannot be ruled out. In science, a tipping point occurs when small changes add up to cause major, more critical change – which can be very sudden, may be irreversible, and can trigger a cascade of other events.

As an example, scientists point to the possibility of the vast Greenland ice sheet slipping into the sea, causing a greater-than-six-metre rise in global sea levels almost overnight. In a slow and steady heating scenario, this ice sheet could take centuries to melt away, but in a tipping point scenario it could collapse suddenly.

If this happens, the city of Sydney, where I live, and home to more than 5 million people, would be partly underwater – and so would many other cities and regions around the globe. Entire low-lying island nations would vanish.

So tipping points, which by their nature are sudden and severe, could be even more destructive than the climate extremes we're already experiencing.

There are several other potential tipping points that scientists commonly highlight, including dieback of the Amazon forests triggered by changing weather patterns, which would kill off the Earth's green lungs. The Arctic region's vast areas of permafrost, literally frozen ground, which could thaw rapidly instead of slowly due to accelerated heating, releasing huge additional amounts of currently trapped carbon into the atmosphere.

There is the potential for interruption to the cross-Atlantic Ocean current, often known as the Gulf Stream, that warms Western Europe by bringing warmer water from lower latitudes around the Gulf of Mexico up into the freezing North Atlantic.

This, in turn, is influenced by fresh water melting into the sea from the Greenland ice sheet. The current's collapse or severe weakening would threaten northern Europe with a much colder future. Scientists are watching this closely already.[9]

Lesley's breakdown of the science is uncompromising. Cyclone (hurricane) intensity is increasing. The water cycle, which drives rainfall through evaporation and precipitation, is intensifying because of rising temperatures. Extreme heat and heatwaves are increasing. Bushfire seasons are lengthening and becoming more severe. She sums up:

> We are in a climate emergency. Our physical and biological world is transforming. We don't have much time. Every fraction of a degree matters. Every year matters. Every choice matters.

The preciseness of this science is startling in its own right. A code red for humanity is stark. The decade 2020 to 2030 is critical if we are to do something meaningful about it, and the clock is ticking. It's not so much the 11th hour as less than one minute to midnight.

2030 and beyond

One thing is for sure about 2030 and beyond. It will be hotter than it is right now. Today's climate science is clear on this. Even if we hold the human-induced global heating trend to a maximum of 1.5°C, we still face more extreme weather, such as heatwaves, than we experience now. And if we don't act decisively in this decade, then average global temperatures will stay on track to rise by between 2.7°C and 3°C by the end of the 21st century, or even worse.

We would be exposing our children and grandchildren to ever more terrifying consequences of runaway climate change. Killer storms. Fires. Acidic oceans. Flooding. Heatwaves. Mass extinctions. Emerging diseases.

And the solution can't be running away. We have only one planet. One home. Nor can we usefully contest the physics of climate change, nor negotiate a better deal for humanity with the planet, nor guilt Mother Earth into just going easy on us. We have to take responsibility.

This emergency is compounded because climate change isn't one-size-fits-all. It isn't equal, and it affects us all differently. Women and children in poorer countries are the most vulnerable, while it's the wealthy countries that have polluted the most. Even within wealthy countries, there is massive inequality too, creating winners and losers in the climate equation.

The solution can't be running away. We have only one planet. One home.

We will only succeed in acting on climate, and fighting for 1.5°C, if we harness the strengths of all citizens of the world, and shape solutions which offer better outcomes everywhere.

Take the Pacific island nations, tiny dots of land in a vast ocean, where rising sea levels are already disrupting the daily lives of inhabitants.

My friend Hilda Heine, former President of the Marshall Islands in the mid-Pacific, is one of the circle of women whom I've met and been influenced by on my climate journey. I've visited Hilda, the Marshallese and their tiny islands deep in the mid-Pacific Ocean, and the contrast between their lives, with their existence-level desperation for climate action, and mine, is stark.

Hilda told me how climate change is impacting the lives of the Marshellese people day to day:

The dining table is affected because we have food plants that are not producing as they used to, because the saltwater intrusion into our soil is affecting a lot of our food plants. People with droughts are worrying about safe drinking water. That's almost on a daily basis. The graveyards are falling into the ocean. Coconut trees are falling into the ocean. A king tide fortunately doesn't come every day, but when it's there, people have to relocate. It may be for weeks while they're cleaning up their front yards or their backyards or putting their homes back together.

Hilda lays the climate inequity bare:

There are rich countries and poor countries, and unfortunately a lot of us in the Pacific are in the latter category. Where we have nothing to contribute to the causes of climate change, and yet we're the ones experiencing the brunt of its impacts. And so as leaders, we all hope that we can create a world where people are not miserable like we are right now. I mean, for countries like the Marshall Islands, we're worried about the future of our country. Whether it's going to be here in 2030. I mean, that's just basic existence.

So here's one thing I know, right here, right now. To be truly progressive, we need to strive for a new world which works better for everyone, including Mother Earth.

While climate change is the headline threat, it's part of an even bigger fundamental challenge for humanity: how our civilisation is to remain sustainable in the 21st century and beyond. The climate crisis is further compounded by the fact that our collective demand for the Earth's resources in a given year now exceeds what the planet can generate in that year.

We need to turn this worsening trend around by 2030, and we can!

Measuring and mitigating change

Lesley Hughes has pointed me to a scientifically based, ready-made measure for how people impact the planet, known as Earth Overshoot Day. Each year, it marks the date when we overshoot what the Earth can sustainably provide.

In 2021, Earth Overshoot Day fell on 29 July. That's for the world as a whole. But there's also a country-by-country breakdown that measures when Earth Overshoot Day would land if everyone in the world lived like a particular country's people.

Micro-nations like the Marshall Islands only have the tiniest of impacts on the global picture. But that's not true of my country, Australia, which is among the top 20 economies in the world. In 2021, for Australia, Earth Overshoot Day fell on 22 March, less than a quarter of the way through the year. Australia's ranking was one of the most extreme outcomes for any country, with only the US, Canada, Kuwait, the United Arab Emirates, Luxembourg and Qatar doing worse. Lesley told me:

We need an understanding of what a finite Earth actually means. We all need to recognise that the earth can only take so much. Earth Overshoot Day, which is the day of the year when we have used all the resources we can afford to in one year, is now about the end of July. If everyone in the world used resources like we do in Australia it would be at the end of March. We need to live within our means.

I wish I could say we were only discovering our twin climate and sustainability crises now, in the 2020s, but the truth is we knew much of it well over a decade ago.

Soon after Al Gore's film *An Inconvenient Truth* helped to trigger my climate journey back in 2006, global attention swung to the release of a much-anticipated report into the economic case for climate action. Top UK economist Sir Nicholas Stern, on a brief from the British Government, forecast a $9 trillion loss in global warming costs for the world, and warned of a small window of 10 to 15 years in which the world could act to change this.[10] Lesley Hughes points out that Stern also described climate change as 'the greatest market failure of all time' – meaning that the people who will suffer the most are those who have done least to cause it.

The mass media finally began to articulate climate change in a way we could all understand. You could hardly read a newspaper, or listen to the radio, or watch television, without there being someone explaining climate change and what we could all do about it. Whether it was the mums and dads at the kids' weekend soccer, or Question Time in the Australian Parliament, climate change was being talked about.

Before this shift, my sense was most people just thought, 'Oh it's okay, the environmental groups are on the case, or governments will fix it.' I know this personally because it's how I used to think. But once I was finally engaged, once I'd internalised the climate challenge as being very much about me and my loved ones, I became hungry to know more and do more. For me, this included joining one of Al Gore's early training sessions for climate campaigners in 2007, through The Climate Reality Project, for which in recent years I've been a mentor rather than a student.

Nearly 15 years later, Gore's 2021 iteration of his now famous climate 'slideshow' and his science-based calculations are mind-blowing. Burning fossil fuels is the largest source of this pollution, and 147 million tonnes is going into the atmosphere each day.[11] That's the equivalent pollution we'd see from running nearly 37 million average-sized petrol-fuelled cars for a year.

Of the 20 hottest years on record, 19 of them have occurred since the year 2002. Warmer air can hold a lot more water vapour, so rain events get bigger, and storms and floods get worse. Extreme weather disasters have cost the global economy $US2.5 trillion in the last decade. The rate of ice melt from the glaciers in the Himalayan mountains has doubled since the year 2000.

The Arctic has now transitioned from helping to limit global heating – including absorbing greenhouse gas pollution out of the atmosphere and reflecting the sun's heat rays back into space off white ice – into being a source of even more pollution. This is due mainly to thawing permafrost releasing methane, the powerful greenhouse gas pollutant, which has been trapped in frozen ground for hundreds of thousands or even millions of years. It's estimated that nearly one-quarter of the northern hemisphere land mass is permafrost,[12] and now its 'permanency' is in serious doubt.

Climate change also is the biggest global health threat of the 21st century, with related pollution already killing nine million people every year. And on the ecosystem health side, we risk losing up to 50 per cent of all land-based species in this century.

We know that staying under 1.5°C requires heroic levels of urgent global action, given we've already passed 1.2°C of average global temperature rise since the Industrial Revolution of two centuries ago. If we haven't locked in staying under 1.5°C of global heating by 2030, our best opportunity is lost, and ever getting back to it becomes incredibly difficult. Hence the 'critical decade'.

The United Nations, through its climate change convention – first established at the landmark Rio Earth Summit three decades ago, in 1992 – is trying to steer the whole world to be 'net zero' for greenhouse gas pollution by 2050. This would have a neutral impact on the concentration of carbon dioxide, methane and some additional minor greenhouse gases in the atmosphere. But that's decades away and, far more importantly, there's a global push to be at least halfway there by 2030.

Lesley Hughes helps us to contextualise all of this science and the evidence before us, and she falls heavily on the side of action rather than more research, analysis and modelling:

> We actually don't just need more and more science. We've got enough science to underpin action right now. In fact, we had enough science 30 years ago. What we really need now is action, technology, will, politics, policy, great economists, great engineers, all of the great passionate people in the community making change. The science provides the rationale for action and the reason for great urgency. It doesn't actually provide the action. It's people like you and what you're doing with 1 Million Women. That's the action, that's just based on the science.

Knowledge is power

So how do we get past the fear, and move into making a difference? Knowing the information compels our attention, but what core characteristics will empower us to act? What drives the determination and the urgency we have to take action this decade on many fronts simultaneously to get us on track for a new, better and genuinely sustainable world?

Here is my own list of ways to stay engaged and ready for the fight.

We need to understand and internalise the immensity of the climate threat. We need to take that knowledge and respond to it with optimism and determination. We need to find our own agency and use our voices to stand up to power and demand action. We need to have conversations with friends and loved ones and share our personal stories on how we feel about climate and we need to connect with and love the Earth, learning from First Nations peoples about living sustainably.

We need to take collective action within our communities. We need to cure ourselves of the twin curses of endemic overconsumption and waste. And we need to pursue personal action every day wherever we can, walking our talk.

We need to take collective action within our communities. We need to cure ourselves of the twin curses of endemic overconsumption and waste.

And I see this happening all around me every day. I see 100 per cent renewable energy coming within our reach and people everywhere questioning today's toxic culture of mass consumerism. People taking action to stop the waste and pollution it causes and holding politicians accountable for their climate inaction and, in particular, I see women leading the way.

These are the things that can lead to our own tipping point, a beneficial one, that totally transforms how we live.

Call to action: First, get yourself a good understanding of climate science, and the kinds of impacts and consequences we are facing. Understand that the critical time for action is in this decade. Feel that knowledge in your heart, not just up in your head. Don't get overwhelmed by the news and the ongoing uncertainty. It's easy to get bogged down in the scientific complexity of it all and to worry that you don't know it all. But getting engaged where you can with determination and passion and knowing that you are powerful is what's important right now. Act and see results and let that propel you forward.

3

OPTIMISM AS A STRATEGY

In late 2018, when 1 Million Women ran our Australia-wide survey of 5000 women, nine out of ten were 'extremely concerned' about the impacts of climate change, and almost as many were feeling actual discomfort from record-breaking heatwaves. And that was before the deadly and destructive 'Black Summer' bushfires in Australia, over the spring and summer of 2019–2020, which were followed by floods (and also the global pandemic).

One in three of the women under the age of 30 who responded to the survey said they were 'reconsidering having children or any more children because of climate change'. This number dropped slightly for women aged between 30 and 39, at 22 per cent compared with 33.4 per cent for the under-30s cohort of women of child-bearing age, but the number was still high enough to surprise me. In fact, it alarmed me, forcing me to confront my own optimism.

I felt deep sadness as we tallied up the responses ahead of that year's national election in Australia. Our survey unpacked a lot of insights into the personal impacts of climate change on women. But the idea of significant numbers of women consciously forgoing children due to climate change was a new narrative for me.

This finding was so deeply personal. I hadn't really heard climate change being discussed so clearly as a life choice issue before, at least not in my circles. Young women were struggling with their decision to start a family in an uncertain world, not knowing what the future might hold. What a terrible burden for anyone to carry.

Reasons for optimism

I was relieved to see that there was positive news coming out of the survey as well. We found that women who already had children overwhelmingly had a renewed focus on doing all they could to live with the least impact on the planet. They were energised to make a difference in the world and to raise their children to be the climate warriors of the future.

The mixed results made me realise how crucial it is for women in particular to be optimistic about the future, to feel a sense of relief and hold onto hope that things can and will be better.

Optimism might not seem like the most obvious response to the existential threat of climate change. But optimism compels us to act decisively. It stops us from sinking into the paralysis of despair.

But I'm not talking about a detached or blind-faith kind of optimism. Just believing that everything will be okay is not the right kind of optimism to have.

The optimism we need must be grounded in action. We can't be passive about it. Not now. Not in this most critical of decades. We can't bury our heads in the sand and think if we just ignore it all and carry on with business as usual, somehow it will pass us by.

We need our optimism to be active. Active optimism puts us on the front foot, able to face our immediate challenges and to see beyond them to long-term sustainable solutions for humanity and the planet.

Active optimism puts us on the front foot, able to face our immediate challenges.

To be strategic, our optimism has to be pragmatic and focused. We need to be alarmed, and then respond constructively. The sheer immensity of our climate challenge compels us to confront horrifying truths, in order to emotionally centre ourselves for the journey ahead, and then channel our emotions decisively into swift action. All of this helps us from sinking into despair or denial.

Optimism is a tonic too. While it's no use pretending that we have nothing to worry about, we can't let ourselves become dominated by pessimism, nor throw our hands up in the air and walk away from the fight.

A positive state of mind is fundamental for our journey. It will never be enough to be merely stoic in the face of the climate crisis. Nor is outrage enough, although we need to channel it to focus our energies on real and timely action. We must have optimism. We must have certainty in our core that things can be made better, and absolute determination to make it so.

Optimism, coupled with determination, is the antidote to fatigue and despair. Optimism builds resilience. It speaks to love and hope. It's vital to motivating and sustaining ourselves through the process of transformation, acting now wherever we can. It's how not to burn out. I know the warning signs of that, when you become overwhelmed and exhausted, and I know how sometimes it just creeps up on you.

While we often speak of climate change as humanity's great existential threat, it's not as though it's a giant asteroid coming at us from outer space without warning, leaving us powerless to respond. Human-induced climate change is here with us now, and we're part of its story, and we do have agency in shaping the outcomes. And that's powerful, if we can harness it.

Optimism is a core ingredient to help us step into our agency, and then sustain it. When we see tangible results being achieved through the actions we are taking individually and collectively it creates the foundation to do more.

Active optimism is created through having conversations with others, engaging with our communities, having a relationship with Mother Earth, and knowing we are not alone. It's through acting in our own life every single day, which could be something as simple as leaving an overpackaged product on the shelf or having zero food waste going into the bin. Through the momentum of our actions and engagement, we create our emotional gravity, and give others the confidence to join in or start their journey too. Even better, when we empower others we are nourished right back, and our gravitational force grows even stronger.

Mixed emotions

While optimism is critical to sustain us in this decade, it's not a magic potion, and there are times when it's okay to let all that grief and worry out. Being an engaged optimist with our hearts and minds doesn't mean we won't ever get overwhelmed by our circumstances, our challenges and the state of the planet. This is really serious stuff. The climate news isn't easy to digest, and sometimes we will find ourselves struggling to navigate every emotion and overcome every fear.

Climate psychologist Dr Bronwyn Gresham explained climate anxiety this way to the 1MW team:

> It is the sense of fear or concern connected to climate change and the ecological destruction that we are experiencing. It's a really legitimate source of stress.
>
> The key coping mechanism for anxiety is positive action. That's what is needed to combat anxiety, but with climate change it is collective action. It's coming together in small groups or joining organisations.

She explains that this can really compensate for the individual culture that we are trying to wake up from. Because when you have an individualised mindset you can feel so alone with this issue.

It means that when we play a role in making a collaborative contribution and if we need to take a breath, we know that the momentum continues because others are still engaged and participating.

Bronwyn talks about the acronym LOVE.

L – listen: listening to the physical signs in our body. It might be our heart rate or feeling tense but also listening to the thoughts that come when anxiety shows up.

O – observe: observing what happens as that emotion moves through you. Trying to diffuse from the emotion.

V – the validation: reminding ourselves that what we are experiencing makes sense. Befriending ourselves and the experience and saying, 'Hey, it's okay to feel this way'.

E – express and experience: making a choice about how we would like to follow this emotion or how to connect with it. In the moment, you might need to take action on climate change or maybe what you need is space and time to resettle.

Our love for our children and families, and our need to do all we can to keep them safe, will always be with us. As will the desperate knowledge that we can't control everything, nor always guarantee positive outcomes all the time.

I become furious every time a politician tells us they are looking after our climate action needs while at the same time they approve yet another coal mine or coal-fired power station, or play statistical tricks with emission reductions.

But my optimism is my counterbalance. It tells me we can change those politicians, through the ballot box if necessary, replacing them with a new breed of climate-aware politicians with determination to drive action.

I also know how easy it is, when faced with climate reality, to feel guilty over not doing enough, or not being able to make enough difference, or being less than perfect. I've gone through periods of despair as well, when it all gets too much, or when the prevailing wall of political apathy and social inertia seems to be insurmountable.

For me, that leads to a deep humility, because if I'm feeling all this in my wealthy-world life, how much worse must it be for our most disadvantaged and marginalised people?

Often we think of emotions such as anger, fear, shame and guilt as being negative and counter-productive, and not useful to our emotional repertoire. With anger, for example, we worry unleashing it will lead to conflict, even violence. Yet it doesn't have to.

Australian social researcher Rebecca Huntley, author of *How to Talk About Climate Change in a Way That Makes a Difference*,[13] tells me 'anger is powerful if we can turn it into positive actions'. Rebecca explains:

Anger can lead to optimism and determination, because when you're angry enough to want to change things, it frees you from apathy and inaction. So it's not a bad place at all. And shame can be good too. If there's a pathway from shame to a sense of obligation and responsibility; to a sense of redress, whether it be from shame or guilt, then that can work really well and becomes a very useful emotion. The trick, it seems, is even when you start from a negative place you can flip it to positive mode and break through from inertia.

I experienced this myself when I was writing this book. During a brief lull in pandemic restrictions in November 2021, I made a last-minute dash to the important United Nations climate summit in Glasgow. Known as COP26, standing for the 26th Conference of the Parties under the United Nations Framework Convention on Climate Change (UNFCCC), it had been postponed for a year because of COVID-19.

For the world, Glasgow was the big opportunity to fight for 1.5°C by locking in national commitments around the Paris Agreement, which dates back to COP21 in Paris, in 2015. For me, Glasgow also was my first real chance in more than two years to reconnect with my circle of women leading on climate change.

Once there, however, I was confronted by mixed emotions. Anger over the Australian Government's lack of interest in setting meaningful emissions cuts by 2030. Sadness that not enough had been done to support those on the frontline of climate change. Grief at what is at stake, like the fate of the iconic Great Barrier Reef, and the threats that rising sea levels pose to hundreds of millions of people. Disappointment in our world leaders for not doing more.

I leaned into the sadness I was feeling, but ultimately my resolve was stronger, and I came away with my optimism refreshed.

Optimism thrives on connection

I marched through the streets of Glasgow with 150,000 others. I marched arm-in-arm with the feminists screaming at the top of my voice, 'We are the feminists, the mighty mighty feminists!' I marched with my dear friend Liane Schalatek, who fills me with joy and strength every time I see her, and was boosted because of the extraordinary power of the people around me, and because I knew I was not alone.

I was part of the bigger global movement. Part of the chorus of voices of women, of First Nations peoples, of youth and Elders, of businesses rising up, all with a shared commitment to act decisively in this decade.

We have to nurture our hope as steadily as we do our optimism. Hope is more a leap of faith than a state of mind or a stratagem. We need to passionately want to change and be hopeful, as well as being optimistic, about achieving our goals. As with optimism, we can't look for hope to materialise out of

We need to passionately want to change and be hopeful, as well as being optimistic, about achieving our goals.

the stars. We can't wait for others to deliver hope. We have to roll up our sleeves, get to work, and create hope through our self-belief and determination to make it so.

I really mean *radical* hope. Hope that helps us to sweep aside sadness, anger, fear, guilt and all the other negative emotions that can assail us. The kind of hope that looks at the pending climate catastrophe, with its potential for the collapse of human civilisation as we know it, and instead sees an amazing opportunity to create a new life and way of being.

Hope like this is genuinely powerful when it's anchored in reality, like the truly extraordinary renewable energy transformation that is sweeping the world already, from solar on the rooftops of our homes, to vast 'farms' of wind towers and solar panels, to the clean electrification of everything – including our vehicles.

Former President of the Marshall Islands Hilda Heine embraces hope as a core part of her *modus operandi*, telling me:

I continue to be hopeful. I think in the absence of hope, then you will really feel depressed. I cannot allow myself to be depressed. So I am hopeful because of humanity and because of the ingenuity of people. I think in the end, we will be able to come together because we care. Most people care for each other. I mean, there are exceptions, but you would think that those with humanity, those with hearts, will overtake the others and that we will come together and work on the solutions for climate change.

For Hilda and her people, climate change and rising sea levels threaten not just daily life, but the future of living at all on the low-lying islands of the tiny Marshallese nation. She hopes technology will throw up new solutions which will help to save her country and others.

> I am also hopeful that something [technological] will happen in the next 10 years, no later than that, that will help with controlling the emission levels and getting us back to where we need to be, in terms of not only sea level rise for us, but also for the heat in the air ... So I have to remain optimistic. And I do that. I tell myself that we will work this out.

I can't talk about climate and optimism without including Christiana Figueres, the hero of the COP21 summit in Paris in 2015, when the world came to the landmark Paris Agreement that aspires to hold global heating to a maximum average of 1.5°C compared with pre-industrial levels. Christiana oversaw the entire process of this historic agreement and is credited with forging a new brand of collaborative diplomacy that saw governments, corporations and activists, financial institutions and NGOs come together to deliver this unprecedented climate change treaty.

The Paris Agreement underpins the framework for climate action in this decade. It compels us to cut greenhouse gas pollution by at least half by 2030; to be on track to effectively eliminate harmful levels of emissions globally by mid-century.

A true champion for 1 Million Women, Christiana lifts my spirits every time I see her. It's why I love her. She has this innate ability to deliver joy and strength to every conversation. She makes you feel like you are the most important person on the planet, capable of doing anything.

In a recent article in *Time* magazine, Christiana cited 'trust' as the greatest resource the world has for achieving post-Paris success, and she warned of its scarcity, and the imperative to rebuild it, starting with us.

'First,' she says, 'we need to rebuild trust in ourselves: trust that we can do what is necessary within the time range determined by science.'[14]

These days, Christiana wears numerous caps: a founder of the Global Optimism organisation, a co-host and driving force of a climate podcast called *Outrage and Optimism*, and the co-author of *The Future We Choose: The Stubborn Optimist's Guide to the Climate Crisis*. This book, written with Tom Rivett-Carnac, is anchored by the theme of 'stubborn optimism' and it portrays the Paris Agreement as a product of this mindset:

Optimism is not soft, it is gritty. Every day brings dark news, and no end of people tell us that the world is going to hell. To take the low road is to succumb. To take the high road is to remain constant in the face of uncertainty. That we may be confronted by barriers galore should not surprise anyone. That we may see worsening climate conditions in the short term should also not surprise us. We have to elect to boldly persevere. With determination and utmost courage, we must conquer the hurdles in order to push forward.[15]

Christiana's brand of stubborn optimism is a model for us all to follow. We can make the choice to tough it out. And we can do it now. I can't overstate how much she has inspired me. When I interviewed Christiana for 1 Million Women's LoveEarth Festival in 2020 she shared her motivational best with me:

First, give up the doom-and-gloom thinking. Get out of despair. Yes, it is absolutely terrible what is happening to nature. And yes, there's moments for grief, but we can't stay in that hole. We have to crawl ourselves out of that hole and move toward hope, towards determination, towards conviction. Knowing that we do have everything that it takes. We have ingenuity. We have the technologies. We know what the policies are. We know what the individual behaviours are. And collectively we can do this.

So we have to put on the mantle of optimism that protects us against the fatalistic and pessimistic thinking that we can't do this. First, be a ferocious and determined optimist. And then we know that there are going to be many challenges ahead, but that we can't stop. We can't just say, 'Oh, well, it's a little bit difficult, or maybe even it's very difficult.' And therefore we would sit back on our couches and twiddle our thumbs and let the world go to hell in a handbasket. No, no, no, no. We are at the point where we can't give up or let up.

Flexing your hope muscles

I know it is not sustainable to expect perfect positivity every single day. But when we are present, when we understand what's at stake, and when we are taking action in our own lives with our families, our friends, and together with our communities, it builds the support structure we need to stay in the optimistic lane.

Like our own bodies, where strength and fitness is about having a strong core, so too is the story of climate resilience. At our very core, if we are strengthened through the actions we are taking, through our interactions with one another, and through knowing we are not alone, then we are building more resilience.

This, in turn, helps to get us through our emotional reactions as we encounter them, and stay strong to face whatever comes next. It's about mindfulness, managing fears around security and safety, and always tipping back from despair and its disempowerment towards optimism and the positive action it inspires.

Make sure you get respite too. Ensure that you're not just constantly feeding your brain with more and more information about what's happening, and how you have to act, and who's in the way, and what you need to do to make even more things happen. Give yourself breaks.

Sometimes, the best action of all is inaction, so you can let your brain switch off, recharge your optimism battery and boost your reservoir of hope. Spend time in nature or green spaces or simply sit down to watch a movie or read a book (personally, I recommend taking time out with a romantic comedy requiring absolutely no brain power whatsoever).

The time to go back into action will come around again soon enough, and if at any time you don't have the headspace for big changes and challenging causes, the practical action you take in your own daily life will keep you going.

Optimism needs to be our emotional baseline to keep ourselves going as agents for change.

Call to action: Find your own optimism zone, and the space to recharge.

- Act in your own life and see the results and the solutions come to life.
- Know you are not alone by having conversations with others. This truly helps build your resilience.
- Don't overload yourself with all the news. Choose your news wisely.
- Don't deny the difficult emotions you are feeling. Lean into them with an openness.
- Walk in nature. Exercise, dance, meditate – do all the things that move your body and help ground you.
- Optimism needs to be our emotional baseline to keep ourselves going as agents for change. None of us can carry the weight of a troubled world on our shoulders 24/7/365. To sustain ourselves, we also need to tap other emotions and experiences too: joy, love, laughter, connection and, sometimes, just letting go for some genuine rest and relaxation.

4

WOMEN'S TRUTH TO POWER

Recently, an image came up on my personal Facebook account, one of the 'memories' the social media platform shows regularly. It was a group photo from the 2018 Global Climate Action Summit in San Francisco, taken at a women's breakfast event I attended. Mary Robinson, former president of Ireland, was the host.

In the picture was Hindou Oumarou Ibrahim from Chad, Africa, an expert in traditional ecological knowledge and Indigenous peoples' adaptation to climate change, and also in mitigation strategies. And Rachel Kyte, then-CEO of the UN-inspired Sustainable Energy for All organisation, and a former World Bank Group Vice President and Special Envoy on Climate Change. Others included Mia Mottley, at the time the newly elected Prime Minister of Barbados; Kathy Jetñil-Kijiner, poet and climate activist from the Marshall Islands; and Neha Misri, co-founder of Solar Sister. Mary Robinson. And me.

The joy and laughter captured in the memory-anchor image from nearly three years earlier, jumped out at me. I was months into a COVID-19 lockdown in Sydney, and it hit me deep in my heart: I was missing the energy of these wonderful, inspiring women. But the image from Facebook told a much deeper story than a bunch of women having a good time at a breakfast. It showed strength in diversity and a deeply felt camaraderie.

This particular breakfast was one of many similar events Mary hosted across the years and I have been so lucky to be part of this circle. It was always a room filled with women. Ten to a table, with a global leader sitting next to a grassroots community activist. All of us equal, sharing our wisdom and expertise as well as our anxieties or concerns. It was a safe space for discussion, allowing conversation to flow and creativity to flourish.

Another such wonderful event was with 100 women. At my table were Graça Machel, Mozambican politician and humanitarian (and widow of the late Nelson Mandela, former

President of South Africa); and Phumzile Mlambo-Ngcuka, Executive Director of UN Women and Under Secretary-General of the United Nations at the time, and a mentor to young women from grassroots organisations around the world.

What an opportunity it was to be with these women, listening, learning and sharing. These events were special, and this particular style of 'women gathering' is one that I have experienced right throughout my journey as founder of 1 Million Women: circular, inclusive, intergenerational, equal.

Women's power is something special

This critical decade for action needs women. Women from every age and demographic, and from all walks of life. It needs us to find our agency and to step into leadership spaces we may never have ventured into before, sometimes because we've never been invited or welcomed in. Spaces we've been shunned from because of misogyny, because of the patriarchy and all of the biases aligned against us.

This decade needs women to marshal our collective power and our emotional intelligence, to gather our networks, and to speak our truth to power. It needs us to be the storytellers, the weavers of new political visions, the positive influencers for a world crying out for fresh ideas.

International Women's Day (8 March) in 2019 had the theme 'Think equal, build smart, innovate for change'[16] and

This decade needs women to marshal our collective power and our emotional intelligence, to gather our networks, and to speak our truth to power.

it was all about tapping into the fresh, relevant thinking of women in order to position them as shapers of innovation and change in our world.

Soon after, a UN-sourced article titled '5 Reasons Why Climate Action Needs Women' proclaimed:

> Everyone should acknowledge the benefits that women bring to climate action so that climate change can be properly addressed. Climate change impacts people differently – in terms of socioeconomic circumstances, disabilities, age and gender. When solutions to climate change address these different realities, they are more effective and their impact ripples through society.[17]

The knowledge that women, and greater gender equality, are key sources of innovation and change also extends strongly to our rising economic power and influence. This is true for those women living more privileged lives in the wealthier nations, and also for rising levels of women's employment, asset ownership and entrepreneurship in less-advantaged parts of the world, including micro-businesses and the micro-lending which overwhelmingly places trust in women. An article from the Asia Society says: 'Worldwide, microfinance loans serve almost 20 million people living in poverty. 74 per cent of these clients are women.'[18]

In 2020, research house Frost & Sullivan published its *Global Mega Trends to 2030*, finding that:

The female economy is poised to outpace the economy of some of the biggest nations in the next five years. With more women entering the workforce, there will be a significant shift in financial and economic power toward women – both in the household and in professional environments.[19]

According to media and audience analytics global leader Nielsen, in a 2020 insights article called 'Wise up to Women,' the market influence trend for women is still very much on the way up: 'By 2028, women will own 75 per cent of the discretionary spend, making them the world's greatest influencers.'[20]

A 2020 article in *Forbes* magazine calls women 'the world's most powerful consumers' already, stressing they have influence as well as power. It recognises women as trendsetters who can shift markets, proposing: 'A good rule of thumb is this: if you want to know where the market is going, follow the women.'[21]

Women and climate are woven together

When it comes to women, climate change and advocacy, I see three main interwoven themes.

One is the imperative for gender equality through greater participation of women in all decision-making, from local to global, however big or small the issue.

The second is the economic power of women through their domination of consumer purchasing and rising impact as employees, employers, investors, businesspeople and entrepreneurs.

And the third is the disproportionate vulnerability of women, and also children, to climate change impacts – not only in the developing world, but also for many disadvantaged and marginalised people living in developed nations.

On gender equality, in this decade, we have to keep pressing for women to be at the table – every table where important decisions are being made. Nowhere is this more true than in our climate crisis.

On gender equality, we have to keep pressing for women to be at the table – every table where important decisions are being made.

Be it a corporate board, a political party, a community group, a ministerial cabinet, a government agency, the judiciary or any other part of the system, women's participation should be normal and expected.

Numerical equality, however, is only a crude quantitative measure of gender equality. What's really important is appreciating the qualitative part: the essence of what it means to have women's voices and views be a part of the equation and recognising the value we bring to the table with our experiences, our views and our voices. Diversity, gender and otherwise, strengthens decision-making.

In the decade-plus history of 1 Million Women, we've often faced a 'why women' question mark. It can be a loaded question. Often other questions sit behind it. Why make climate change another battleground for gender equality? It's an environmental issue, isn't it? Is this just a feminist thing? Or a mother thing?

The most obvious riposte is: why not women? We're more than half the global population. Equality is our human right. And while the 'why women' question still gets asked, it now gets answered comprehensively in key global organisations like the United Nations and the World Economic Forum, with a clear message that I'm paraphrasing: the world needs women to be engaged, participating and leading – in this decade.

This urgency is being embraced at a civic level globally, with women at the forefront of action. The C40 Cities organisation is an impressive movement made up of 100 mayors from around the world, women and men, whose cities are committed to halving their emissions in this decade. One of its key initiatives is the Women4Climate program, a global mentoring initiative that supports and enhances women's leadership in all sectors, creating a powerful global community of over 600 women engaged in solving the climate crisis.[22] I'm a mentor for the program, which says:

> As we look to address the greatest challenge humankind has ever faced, we do so with one of the greatest possible resources: womankind. Empowering women is key to creating cities and communities that are clean, safe and economically vibrant. This is true not only because women make up 50 per cent of the global population but also because women are powerful advocates for solutions to long-term problems like climate change.[23]

My friend Lorena Aguilar, a veteran in the gender and climate space, has devoted her life to empowering women and fighting for climate justice. I love her dearly. The work she does is so important. Lorena was recently Costa Rica's Vice Minister of Foreign Affairs, and among many roles also served for nearly two decades as Global Senior Gender Adviser for the International Union for the Conservation of Nature (IUCN).

Thirty years ago, she recalls people thinking she was crazy to talk about the link between gender and women's empowerment and the environment on every front – biodiversity, drylands, wetlands conservation, protected areas, climate change. But she made it her lifelong commitment, educating the environmental movement and the women's movement.

She has worked with women from all around the world and has helped shine a light on the innovative, transformational value of what women bring to the table. She has helped bring so many women into key climate forums so their voices can be heard and their solutions can be seen. This is how Lorena explained it when talking to me for the book:

> Women are a source of innovation when it comes to survival. It is illogical not to bring everybody into this equation. All of us, youth, women, Elders, all of us. And in the combination of all that diversity and all that knowledge is like the correlation with an ecosystem. The ecosystems that are stronger are diverse, and they build their strength in diversity. That's why women are important, because we bring diverse perspectives; we bring knowledge and different powers into these processes.

The view from the developing world with its widespread poverty and inequality reinforces the immensity of our challenge. It's commonly stated that 70 per cent of the world's poor are women. Eliminating extreme poverty by the end of this decade is one of the UN's 17 Sustainable Development Goals (SDGs) for its Decade of Action, between 2020 and 2030, which seeks to mobilise transformative action for sustainability globally and locally, through communities everywhere.[24] Gender equality is another of the SDGs, further highlighting its importance, and so is climate action.

Women are also disadvantaged when it comes to food security, our most basic of human needs. In 2013, the UN's World Food Program estimated that 60 per cent of the world's hungriest people were women, because when poor households experience food shortages, women tend to go without food so their family members can eat, which results in malnutrition and other health problems.[25] Globally, women produce half of the world's food but are around 11 per cent more likely than men to report food insecurity.

This can be relieved by investing more in women, with the UN's Food and Agriculture Organization finding that:

If women who run small farms were given equal access to resources as men, their yields would grow by 20 to 30 per cent, increasing the total agricultural production of low-income countries from 2.5 to 4 per cent. Although this number may appear small at first glance, it would reduce the rate of undernourishment in the world, lifting up to 150 million people out of hunger ...

Although traditional gender roles assign women much of the labour associated with food production, structural inequalities deny them ownership and decision-making powers, which renders them more vulnerable to food insecurity.[26]

Because women often lack the same access to resources and opportunities as men, they are disproportionately impacted by the effects of climate change.

What an extraordinary statistic, highlighting the critical role women can play in agriculture and rural economies across the world. Yet because women often lack the same access to resources and opportunities as men, they are disproportionately impacted by the effects of climate change. This limits their productivity and ability to care for themselves and others.

The particular vulnerability of women and children to climate change-related harm has to be a core theme for our critical decade too. The UN clearly recognises this, with a *UN Chronicle* article saying:

Women are increasingly being seen as more vulnerable than men to the impacts of climate change, mainly because they represent the majority of the world's poor and are proportionally more dependent on threatened natural resources.[27]

As the first woman ever to hold the position of President of the Marshall Islands, Hilda Heine has so much lived experience as a small island nation leader in the climate firing line. What I've learned from knowing Hilda is immeasurable. Several years ago – when I was a guest in her fragile, beautiful country, which is a sprawling chain of volcanic islands and coral atolls in the central Pacific Ocean – she opened my eyes to the climate reality for the Marshallese.

I was there for a Micronesian women's conference, bringing together representatives from a number of small island nations. The week-long conference was all about their particular issues: drought, flooding from rising sea levels, threats to food and water supply, and a rise in domestic violence which also was being attributed to climate change. So often when people and their societies come under stress, it's women and children who end up suffering disproportionately, and the climate crisis is no exception.

The UN recognises this explicitly, for both developing and developed world societies, with a 2019 article saying:

Climate change is recognised as a serious aggravator of gender-based violence. Around the world, climate change-induced crises have also been shown to worsen domestic violence, whether in relation to sexual and reproductive health or discrimination against Indigenous communities. Violence against women is not limited to developing countries. Research conducted into natural disasters, such as bushfires and droughts, in one developed country (Australia) found that they have increased the risk of domestic violence in rural regions. One of the reasons for this is the social and psychological pressure arising from loss of income resulting from the growing impact of climate change on the agricultural sector. Climate action is therefore an essential component in the ongoing fight to eliminate violence against women and girls. The world also needs greater involvement of women in climate action, for example by putting an emphasis on gender mainstreaming in the policymaking process.[28]

From her frontline position in the Pacific, Hilda sees both the vulnerabilities of women and also their strengths when they unite in awareness and action:

This is an issue for all of humanity. We can't look at this as our own little world. We're part of a big world. Just the fact that 'I'm okay' doesn't mean everyone else is too. We need to be mindful of other people's existence.

I asked Hilda what it was like to be the first woman to run her country, and how it informed her own climate fight. She told me:

What I am pretty sure about is that being a woman president, I think the conversation changed. There was focus on gender issues where it wasn't there before, even in allocation of resources. We consider what or whether things are better for or good for women in terms of the actions that we're taking, and in terms of policies. So I'm pretty sure there were changes in how things were done.

But the fact is that we're still few in numbers and we don't have a lobby group to push, even at the leadership level. You still see the men's club dominating and they are strong because they come in numbers, whereas we women are outside that club and we're very few and we cannot be as influential.

Using our power to create a better world

Hilda has helped me to understand that when it comes to climate change, gender equality isn't an end in itself, but rather a means to a bigger end: a better and more sustainable world.

Women don't need to be granted equal rights and participation just to tick a box for gender equality at UN summits or anywhere else. We need it for ourselves, and for everyone, men included, so we can speak our truths in the forums that matter and contribute as equals to shaping and delivering better outcomes.

It's by no means a stretch to say that a lack of women holding equal power in key decision-making roles continues to hold back action on climate change and global sustainability,[29] right when we need us most.

Fabian Dattner is an Australian leadership specialist, CEO of the Dattner Group, who is well known to many for the work she does. She is also the heart and soul and founder of the Homeward Bound Project, a global initiative to elevate the visibility of women in STEMM leading a sustainable future. As part of the project, women are taken on remarkable and life-changing journeys to Antarctica. To date, more women have gone to Antarctica as a result of Homeward Bound than in the history of polar exploration.

Fabian is deeply thoughtful about leadership and is passionately concerned about making sure women in particular are involved in the big decisions for our future. Not simply for equality reasons, but pragmatically, in order to actually achieve sustainability. This is how she breaks it down.

Here are two things I believe to be true:

1. The belief based on really good evidence that the practice of the current leadership is moribund. It's out of kilter with the world. The model we have is an old military model. It's structurally hierarchical and it's not agile. People with the money and the position and the geographical status control the world. That's a model of leadership that is hundreds of years old in a world that is changing.

2. As a leadership specialist and activist I have a deep worry at the pernicious absence of women at the leadership table in volume not as a proposition of equity but as an issue of sustainability. Equity is an assumed starting point but it's not sufficient to change our approach to the practice of leadership. I actually think women are what the planet needs right now. We need to be talking about intersectionality and inclusion of all people. And guess who is in charge to give us the best shot at that? Women, and by our nature we will create that environment.

Mary Robinson and her influential events have taught me that, as women, sometimes we first have to create our own tables. It's a way of standing up to incumbent power, and of rejecting the patriarchy.

My earliest experience with one of Mary's events was when 1 Million Women won our first big award, in 2013. It was COP19, held in Warsaw, Poland, and the award was given to us as part of the United Nations Momentum for Change's 'Lighthouse Awards for the Beacons of Hope' – with the recipients being women's organisations demonstrating carbon reduction solutions for our planet.

Going to that COP, my first, had a profound effect on me. It introduced me to the wider world of climate activism. It inducted me into the global women's climate movement. It helped me better understand the way climate negotiations are conducted at this global scale.

It opened my eyes to the much bigger women's global climate fight: making women's voices heard in traditionally male-dominated climate negotiations forums, and throughout political systems across this planet. Women uniting to collectively take it up to the patriarchy, speaking our truth to their power, and exposing the lack of diversity among decision-makers. I asked Mary about this particular style of women's leadership:

I think women's leadership is different and much more thoughtful in ensuring a diversity of voices. And I learned in the climate context, first of all, the importance of getting women leaders to engage because when I went to my first climate conference, COP, which was Copenhagen, relatively recent to the climate issue myself, and it was very technical, very scientific and very male.

So we worked on the gender action plan. We realised how important it was to let those urgent voices of Indigenous women, of grassroots women, of young women, frankly, to be at the table. We needed them as delegates. So we persuaded women ministers who are part of our network to have as part of their delegation Indigenous women, grassroots women, young women and that had a huge impact because those voices with our delegate's badges were at the table and they silenced the room.

Women have a way of leading that is problem-solving, that is listening, and that is less hierarchical and more consultative. And women have an empathy for being discriminated against. We all know what it's like to have a certain amount of discrimination, even if we get to the top as either heads of state or prime ministers or ministers. It's probably been a tougher route. And we remember the difficulties and that creates more compassion and empathy.

And so I do feel that women who are in top positions are much more inclined to speak openly about the fact that they have problems or they may have difficulties or they may have made mistakes. And women are much more open to admitting that. And that's a strength.

Mary shares a beautiful example of these tables of women that she hosted, working as they should.

I can tell a story that Hindou Oumarou Ibrahim tells. We arranged this dinner at these tables and we had the participation of different people at different tables. Hindou was chair of the Indigenous Peoples Forum, and she was in despair because although the Paris Agreement had indicated, especially in the preamble, the importance of the Indigenous voices, she wasn't getting support. She came to our event, and she found, at different tables, different ministers. She also found other civil society and Indigenous and business participants.

She went to the ministers and said, 'Please help me. Tomorrow we have an important meeting. Will you be there at the table?' And several of those women responded, particularly a young Luxembourg Minister who went out of her way and was at the table when it mattered. I met Hindou a day or two later and her face was smiling. She said, 'Mary, you have no idea how important it was that you hosted that dinner and enabled me to have access to these women ministers.'

Leading social researcher Rebecca Huntley sees an 'ethic of care', like a sixth sense, which women have. She says women are thinking about their children, their grandchildren, or future generations more broadly. They're thinking about their legacy for other generations, and Rebecca paints this as being a very different conversation from the one men typically have, telling me:

> Women often articulate their concern around climate and environment in relation to those things. Often they are more concerned about the nexus between health, mental and physical health, and climate. The second thing is that it's absolutely true that women, young women, particularly, are really excellent climate communicators.

Diversity matters, clearly, but it's a lot more than an ethical requirement. In business, there's been growing recognition for years that greater diversity – especially gender and ethnic diversity – is more than just a moral good. It leads to better decision-making overall, and it boosts the financial bottom line too – according to a 2015 McKinsey report from the UK, which concluded that diversity 'makes sense in purely business terms'.[30]

The World Economic Forum (WEF), in a 2021 article, highlights the crucial importance of women's leadership for addressing climate change and other crises, while warning that COVID-19 has actually set back representation of women leaders by 68 per cent across the board.

Media coverage of the WEF's annual Global Gender Gap Report in 2021 further highlighted the problem. Pre-pandemic, it had been estimated it would take nearly a century, 99.5 years, to reach global parity for a range of important criteria. Post-pandemic, this had blown out to 135.6 years because COVID-19 had hit women on average harder than men, with women's jobs proving more vulnerable in lockdowns and an even greater burden of household responsibilities being foisted on to women.[31]

On climate specifically, we can see how women who have been running countries or fulfilling other leadership roles in government are associated with more ambitious climate policies. A 2019 article in the *Yale Climate Connection* highlights a study conducted by Australia's Curtin University, which examined 91 countries and found that greater female representation in national parliaments does lead countries to adopt more stringent climate change policies.[32]

So real gender parity in politics still seems a far-off dream. The WEF's 2021 Global Gender Gap Report found the political gender gap won't close completely for another 145.5 years, based on current trends, pointing out this was a 50 per cent increase from the estimated 95 years in the same report just one year earlier. So now we also have to catch up on the pandemic's setbacks.

Picking up the slack on gender equality

At the time of my early writing for this book, in September 2021, UN Women reported that globally there were only 26 women serving as heads of state or government, in 24 countries; and, at the current rate, gender equality in the highest positions of power will not be reached for a further 130 years.[33]

Only 25 per cent of all national parliamentarians are women, up from 11 per cent in 1995.[34] In 2015, women headed just 12 per cent of federal environmental ministries worldwide.[35]

In business, meanwhile, in January 2022, only just over 6 per cent of CEOs on America's S&P 500 corporate index were women.[36] If climate action moves as slowly as gender equality in the corridors of power, then humanity is in deep trouble.

To hold our 1.5°C line we have to turn this around, in this decade, because women's leadership and involvement are needed at the climate action frontline more than ever. Women have solutions. Women know how to turn knowledge into action. We are visionaries and powerful organisers. Women have ingenuity and creativity and can lead the way, and this is being demonstrated right across the world.

But there's more to be done. The truth of the matter is, we need more women leading. We need *more* women turning knowledge into action, and organising and using our ingenuity to foster movement on climate in every space and place of society.

We need *more* women turning knowledge into action, and organising and using our ingenuity to foster movement on climate in every space and place of society.

Initiate conversations around climate change

This decade needs us all to bring our truth to power through the actions we are taking, through the conversations we are having, through the people we can influence, through making our voices heard, and through the support we give to other women to help them lead and find their voices too.

Having conversations about climate action helps you jump into your agency and mobilise others. Here are a few tips:

- A conversation can happen anytime, anywhere.
- Bringing up a climate news story as a conversation starter can be a great way to launch into the conversation.
- Find your personal anecdote or story (more on this in Chapter 6: Become the Storyteller). Stories are a powerful way to engage others on big issues. Share what made you care about the climate crisis or how it impacts your life.

- Have a few facts and statistics up your sleeve as this can ground your personal experiences and add authority.
- Every conversation you have will, inevitably, be different so make sure you ask the other person what they think about climate change and listen to what they have to say. This will help you engage with their values and will also make the other person feel heard.
- Frame your conversation with optimism and strength and bring in some easy actions and solutions so there are tangible things to focus on.
- Think about who you are having the conversation with. Speak to people who are on the fence or want to do more but just don't know how. They'll be more receptive to discussion and you can help move them to action.
- Remind people how important they are in this decade of climate action.

We can all find our courage to lead, and internalise how powerful we can be. As women, we need to lead *our* way and not try to play the same game as men. We have to get ourselves outside the patriarchal framework that has dominated our society's power structures for so long. Simply defined, speaking truth to power means standing up for what's right.

> **Call to action:** Participate wherever you can. It all counts, however big or small the forum, and however minor or major the decisions being made. Don't wait to act. Just jump in. Action is, in itself, leadership. Find your voice, stand up and speak up, and build your own stories for change. It takes courage and bravery and conviction, but when you can unlock your own climate stories, you will speak your own truth, which will resonate with someone else. Do all you can to support gender equality as both a basic good and a path to sustainability.

Simply defined, speaking truth to power means standing up for what's right.

5
YOUNG WOMEN RISING

Just in the last few years, I have witnessed evidence of leadership and female empowerment on a level like no other. It's the rise of young women.

This is a story of young people, but especially young women, who are rising up around the world. Their determination to demand real action on climate change is a palpable force. They are hugely impatient with old power structures, especially when they are pale, male and stale.

I got up close to this youth phenomenon in 2019, when I went to New York to be part of the UN Climate Action Summit. I timed my arrival so I could participate in the global climate strike beforehand. It was in September, early in the northern hemisphere autumn, and over four million people protested that day in coordinated marches around the world – at over 4500 locations, in 150 countries.

It was the biggest climate strike in history, and power was being confronted with every step of every marcher. There in New York, in Trump's America, I marched with 250,000 others through the streets, finally converging in Battery Park with its 10 hectares of public space located at the southern tip of Manhattan Island. A young girl, Marisol Rivera, age 13, was one of the event's organisers. During Hurricane Sandy, when Marisol was 6 years old, the roof of her house in New York's Bedford-Stuyvesant neighborhood collapsed, nearly hitting her. Commenting about the march, she said, 'I feel hopeful seeing the power of all these people here today, calling to end fossil fuels and build a better future for us.'[37]

Fittingly, given the mass focus on global heating, it was a blistering hot day. We were filled with excitement and anticipation, however, because the speakers addressing the crowd (all of whom were amazing young people) at the end of the march included global climate activism phenomenon Greta Thunberg, from Sweden, who sparked the school strike movement when she began protesting alone outside the Swedish parliament in 2018. Through her solitary protest at parliament when she was 15, Greta shifted global awareness and behaviour.

For the journey to the climate strike in New York and to speak at the UN Climate Action Summit, at the age of 16, Greta had shown her fresh and uncompromising storytelling by refusing to fly to America – she travelled by solar-powered boat across the Atlantic instead. We waited four hours for Greta to come to the stage. When she eventually did, it was like the Beatles had just arrived, miraculously transported from the 1960s.

The crowd went crazy. Some young people right up the front fainted from the heat and joy and the adrenaline of Greta being there on stage in front of them. I was at the back of the crowd, getting light relief from a slight breeze, while I watched a sea of people united by the common goal to fight for humanity. I was amazed at how this one girl, yet to become an adult, had galvanised this extraordinary momentum.[38]

Power figures visibly struggle to know how to respond to her voice and fiery rhetoric, backed as it is by a global youth network. At COP26 in Glasgow, when thousands of young people took to the streets, Greta denounced the slow-moving conference negotiations as 'blah blah blah'. So what is this 'Greta phenomenon'? And is it more than just coincidence she is a young woman?

To me, it's actually not *her* phenomenon per se. It's much bigger than that. It's young people all over the world stepping into their agency, finding their voices to speak youth truth to mainly old power – and it's phenomenal to witness. Young people are angry and that brings out a raw honesty which is rare in a world of spin. It's infectious. And it is overwhelmingly young women who are leading the way.

***

Young people are angry and that brings out a raw honesty which is rare in a world of spin. It's infectious.

***

A new kind of youthquake

Young girls in their teens who are eloquent and fierce are holding politicians and corporations accountable for their climate inaction. They're doing it for the sake of their own futures and those of generations coming after them. They are uncompromising, and they also are great storytellers.

Young women not yet out of high school themselves are organising school strikes of thousands at a time. They are fighting for their survival, and Rebecca Huntley tells me it is no surprise young women are leading the youth climate movement around the world, including in First Nations communities, because of their natural communications skills, their willingness to share and their savviness on social media. They can find ways to mobilise everyone: parents and grandparents, aunties and uncles, colleagues and friends.

Young people are making the rest of us lift our game. It's the rise of youth which is putting intolerable pressure on governments. The young in their millions are providing the loudest voice. The many millions of school strikers from every corner of the planet are stepping out in front. Young people are filled with outrage, betrayal and frustration, and they are channelling it in a way that's working.

People across generations are marching in solidarity with the youth of the world and we're stepping into our own agency while we do it. Youth's reach extends to the corridors of traditional power as well, because political and corporate powerbrokers often have their own children and grandchildren. These are voices in their hearts as well as their heads, who are even harder for them to ignore or deny than mere citizens with a vote to cast or a dollar to spend.

I have learned so much from the young women and men around me. They have made me even more determined. My own 1 Million Women team of young women makes me want to always be a better leader.

There are so many examples emerging from this surge of youth involvement. Young women whom I have had the privilege of meeting, such as Vanessa Nakete, the Ugandan climate justice activist and author; Adenike Oladosu from

Nigeria, who is fighting for Lake Chad; and my friend, Indigenous campaigner Tish King, a Torres Strait Islander from Australia's tropical north, who is stepping up and leading the way for her Elders:

> Often I was the only Torres Strait Islander in the room, if I wasn't the only black person in the room as well. And so in this space, I've always had to adapt, evolve, decolonise, in a nonaggressive way. It is my cultural responsibility to use my skills and education to help amplify frontline stories and be able to have these critical conversations with likeminded people. As a young woman, I know that it is time to take on the responsibilities that many of our Elders and Traditional Owners have advocated for our communities and for culture to exist.
>
> We hold these truths to be so self-evident that all men and women are created equal. But we continue to see systemic and racial inequalities, where I know that if I had one life on this Earth, it would be to ensure that my people, our people, First Nations people continue to survive and thrive, for more generations to come.

When I was invited into the C40 Cities Women4Climate program as a mentor, I joined a network dedicated to empowering young women to be 'the climate heroines who are building the world of tomorrow'. Launched in 2017, the program declares:

> Women leaders played a pivotal role in negotiating the Paris Agreement on climate change in 2015, and will be crucial to its success in the future. Now more than ever, enhancing women's participation and leadership will be critical to securing a healthy, prosperous and sustainable future for us all.[39]

Hindou Oumarou Ibrahim, environmental activist and member of the Mbororo community in Chad, also is a mentor for the program. She sums it up beautifully: 'Women's leadership is built on educating young girls. We have to tell them that they can be whatever they want, whether a doctor, scientist, community leader or minister.'[40]

A green economy for the next wave of workers

Green jobs are another imperative for young people in this decade. We need to be upskilling and reskilling and training young women and men. My friend Lorena Aguilar now works freelance on climate solutions with women in Latin America, with a particular interest in empowering young women. She shared a story that's a wonderful example of young women doing the jobs that count for the future.

In Paraguay, a group of young women are thriving. In a protected area, in one of the few forests that remain in one of the poorest countries in South America, poverty-stricken Indigenous communities have created a learning centre which is attached to the reserve.

Young Paraguayan girls get into this educational system, and come out with a university degree related to the use and management of natural resources. What they are doing is amazing, because now the people who are doing all the management of this forest in the reserve are these girls. They develop and sell organic products, and invite tourism, but every effort is directed towards the girls, and to developing the capacity of these future sustainability agents of Paraguay.

Rachel Kyte, Dean of The Fletcher School of Law and Diplomacy at Tufts University and former Special Representative of the UN Secretary-General and CEO of Sustainable Energy for All, has been a source of inspiration to me for many years, and I adore her friendship.

Rachel told me Australia can lead the way on youth engagement and education:

In every community, young people need to be trained and educated for the jobs that are going to be in this green economy. And if we are walking into communities, even into coal-mining communities, and saying we've got your back and not investing in their skills for the future, we're letting them down.

And the Australian government can't afford to let Australian young people down because we need Australian young people. The whole of Asia needs Australian young people. So we're going to go green. We've got to go green with those technical skills in communities for young Australians right now.

Around the world, there are more than 1.8 billion young people between the ages of 10 to 24 – the largest amount of youth ever.[41]

We are all witnessing this rise of youth unfold before our very eyes, and we must all be present for them. Every generation must grab hold of this outpouring of energy from our youth and harness it. Every generation must fight for the generations to come. Every generation must be present.

Call to action: From a young woman who stepped into her agency, found her voice and realised her power – Briana Kennedy, our head of digital at 1MW:

When we care and act on climate, we are taking our future into our own hands. No matter how large or small

Every generation must grab hold of this outpouring of energy from our youth and harness it. Every generation must fight for the generations to come. Every generation must be present.

our actions are, they all add up. If you are a young person just starting on your journey, living climate action starts with doing little things like swapping clothes with friends instead of buying new, avoiding fast fashion and microtrends, ditching single use plastics and saving food from going to waste. Start with one simple action and once you're comfortable with that choose another. Do one more thing today than you did yesterday and more again tomorrow. Build your confidence through the actions you take.

As young people, we deserve a say in the future. The youth are rising and we are holding our own. Register to vote the moment you can and use that vote for climate action. Join a climate action group or environmental group at your school. Together we are powerful and loud. March in the big climate marches and school strikes. Join @1millionwomen and be part of our new campaign #1MREADY and take that to your school. It's all about doing all we can right here, right now.

Being around other passionate young people can help you find your voice. We all have a story. Movements are built by sharing our stories and connecting to other people through shared experiences. Take the things that make you care about climate action and let your friends and family know. The Influence you have in your immediate circle is immense. Even if you reach just one person, that's one more person to hold this shared responsibility for the future of the planet.

Most importantly, build your relationship with Earth. Wanting to do everything we can to commit to climate action is natural when we've connected deeply with Mother Earth in our hearts.

Remember, we are not in this alone.

6

BECOME THE STORYTELLER

When I was creating 1 Million Women, I didn't know much about climate policy, and only snippets of the science – so it was challenging. I had no idea who Australia's Environment Minister was at the time. But I knew my story, and it was real. I had changed my daily life, stopped a lot of my pollution from going into the atmosphere in the process, and found my voice. Once I owned my story, all the reasons and excuses I had for not acting dissipated, and I was ready to step into the unknown.

As Professor Lesley Hughes told us earlier, we don't actually need more of the science. That case is made. What we do need is action galore, and to drive this we need relatable storytelling. Stories help spread the word about solutions, and the actions which can be taken by people everywhere in this decade.

We need to find our voices and share our stories – our personal truths. Our raw and honest account of how we feel about climate. We need more conversations about climate in which we really connect to others, and the most powerful way to do that is to tell our own authentic stories.

I see now that it is only through the amazing experiences I've shared as part of my 1 Million Women journey that I've become a better storyteller. I've become more confident in raising my voice. I'm capable of going into any room, no matter who's in it, and engaging an audience with storytelling.

I am still nervous when I stand on stage or sit on a panel (not sure that will ever go away). But my confidence shines through when I can settle back and tell my real and honest story, and I can always feel that moment when I am resonating with the audience. There is that 'listening with intent' feeling in the atmosphere.

I know public speaking can be terrifying, but we don't all need to stand in front of crowds to lead. We just need to connect with someone else and change their way of thinking or influence them to act, or help them find their voice.

Finding a voice on climate

So what are the barriers we face, to tell our story, to lead and to step into unfamiliar spaces? I think for many of us it goes like this.

When we don't know enough about a subject, we feel disempowered to do anything about it – leading us to shy away and do nothing. I know that this was my own experience before I started 1 Million Women. Climate change seemed too overwhelming. And what could one person really do to make a difference, right?

I felt embarrassed about speaking up when I wasn't an expert on the topic. I didn't know enough about it all, and I didn't want others to know I didn't know. So it was much easier to just stay quiet and do nothing. Keep your head down and hopefully no-one will notice.

Rebecca Huntley suggests that self-identity is another barrier to entry. She explained to me that people who don't identify as environmentalists or climate activists can feel it's not their role or job to participate.

I know this barrier well. I used to think: 'I'm a cosmetics manufacturer, not an environmentalist. It's not my job to be saving the planet. I'll leave that to someone else.'

One of the early steps I took towards creating my own narrative was to surround myself with likeminded people.

Participation helps reinforce and refine the mission. Jumping in and listening played a huge role in me finding my voice.

Women, mainly, but not exclusively, who would validate what I was doing while also steering me towards the best path.

Participation helps reinforce and refine the mission. Jumping in and listening played a huge role in me finding my voice. There was no ego involved, just a sense of being sisters through purpose; literally sitting around my kitchen table being genuinely creative and mutually supportive.

We wanted to build something special, a new type of climate movement which would speak to women, harnessing their strengths, empowering them to act in their lives, and helping them all to step up and find their voices. It would be a movement filled with heart and storytelling and collective power.

I see this sense of camaraderie almost every day on the ever-evolving 1 Million Women journey. There is a common thread binding us as women. We are fighting for a common cause: in this case, for the sake of humanity and all species; and for all children on earth and for the generations to come.

Having this kind of support and validation helps you step into new spaces, and to go where you never thought you'd go before. It's also about believing in yourself and doing things, no matter how small they may be, because you know that action is built on action. When you have one experience behind you, even the smallest of successes, it is so much easier to move on to the next thing.

I've learned that storytelling is the most powerful way of leading. When we are stepping into our agency, there is nothing more powerful than storytelling as an instrument for change. It brings out our truths, so we can speak up to power.

I know that I personally will forget facts within seconds of hearing them, but I'll remember information when it has a personal story attached. Stories emotionally connect with others. They help people identify with our journeys. They are real. Honest. Our stories give others the strength to lead too.

Powerful vested interests like the coal and gas industries have their own messaging – untruthful, but enabled by deep corporate pockets.

For example, Naomi Oreskes is a world-renowned geologist and historian, and a leading voice on the role of science in society and the reality of human-induced climate change. In the much-celebrated 2011 book she co-authored with Erik M. Conway, *Merchants of Doubt*, strong parallels are drawn between the corporate manipulation of science and truth by the tobacco industry on one hand and the fossil fuel industry on the other. It says at one point:

Global warming would become the mother of all environmental issues, because it struck at the very root of economic activity: the use of energy. So perhaps not surprisingly, the same people who had questioned acid rain, doubted the ozone hole, and defended tobacco now attacked the scientific evidence of global warming.[42]

The amount of corporate spending on advertising to the masses and lobbying behind closed doors can change public perception on climate change in a big way. So we need our stories to counter theirs, and we need to outscore them with truth and passion, so that those in power realise that the spin isn't actually working.

Storytelling from the heart

When you tell your story, and feel it connect, there's a different flow of energy which comes through in the telling. This energy connects to our hearts, not just our heads, and it's endlessly renewable too.

We must connect with people's hearts as well as their minds. If we only speak to the head, then it is much easier for our audiences to close their minds and mentally shut the door to action.

In this critical decade on climate, we must connect with people's hearts as well as their minds. If we only speak to the head, then it is much easier for our audiences to close their minds and mentally shut the door to action. When stories travel to our hearts, this is when we can truly connect and cut through.

I do a lot of public speaking, and I have never shown a slide deck. I just talk, I want my audiences to focus on what I am saying and nothing else. I talk about how I got the point on climate change – about the fact that I am not a scientist, nor a traditional green role model. Far from it. I used to be part of the problem!

I am, however, a citizen of this planet obliged to do all I can for the sake of humanity and future generations, and all living species on earth. My story is a story of change, and demonstrating change is powerful. And once I realised I was powerful, through every choice I was making, my voice followed. I felt purpose in my heart, and I was able to step into my agency.

Annette Miller, a Rembarrnga/Dalabon Elder from Arnhem Land in the north-east corner of Australia's Northern Territory, uses her position to empower young Aboriginal women. She shared her piece of storytelling with me.

Women's time is right now, and as an Elder it is my responsibility to teach young women and men how to care for Country. I grew up in the middle of Arnhem land. I grew up traditionally. I grew up in the bush, running wild and living in shelters and there was a lot of rocky country, waterways, billabong and wildlife. Slowly years went by and there was a lot of destruction and a lot of damage done to the environment.

What we face today globally with global warming is the biggest issue and I saw a lot of the men who couldn't say that so that power transferred to women. As strong as Aboriginal men were, women were stronger at home, where I come from. So I now teach young women to find their voice. We are pushing the younger generation to say no to fracking and mining.

We have created a women's ranger workers program where young women are learning what healthy burning means. Learning what healthy Country means. Outstations and remote communities are learning culture and good management of waterways, woodlands and forests because if that goes, the birds go too.

I've never been a person that wanted to be under the spotlight. It just happened that way. If you are a person that lives off the land, to have the connection to the land and your cultural heritage, your cultural background will need you later in life. That's what happened with me and other women saw how I presented myself and spoke up and explained things and how I talked in a couple of languages.

They saw a strong woman. A person I had never been and now am. A person from the middle of nowhere. When I first worked with the rangers I saw young women who couldn't talk. They were a shell that wouldn't come out and now these young women are outspoken.

Of course there are always barriers, internal and external, which we have to push through. Finding your own stories doesn't mean you'll never feel the barriers and self-constraints women often feel burdened by: Am I good enough in my own life? Am I an imposter who someone will call out? Is what I have to say even worthy of sharing?

But we can leave all this baggage behind; take a deep breath, exhale, and let it go. Because it can get exhausting consuming ourselves with these thoughts.

I remember a weekend workshop I did with an extraordinary group of women. These women have since become lifelong friends, but at the time of this gathering, I was consumed by feelings of personal inadequacy: Maybe it was a mistake that I was even part of the group? Maybe they got the wrong Natalie? Who was I to presume to engage and influence them?

Then, during one of the sessions, we all shared our feelings, and I discovered many of the women in the circle felt exactly the same way, assailed by their own cocktails of self-doubt. It helped me, when I was struggling in those early days to overcome the inner voice questioning my ability to lead, to realise how many other women felt the same way.

So in a strangely effective way, this experience boosted my confidence rather than fuelling my insecurities, and I evolved.

Stories are a part of the fabric of our resilience

Finding your story through the actions you take will build your confidence to speak up and confront power. I promise you that. And when we are connecting with others, bringing joy and hope, that is powerful too. We will always connect better with whoever we are talking to if we can populate our 'telling' with optimism, solutions and ways to act.

Finding your story through the actions you take will build your confidence to speak up and confront power.

I always try to infuse my messaging with hope and joy, wrapped around the serious challenges we are highlighting, with a clear call to action. I don't dodge the urgency, or the importance, but nor do I wallow in misery.

Rebecca Huntley tells me:

There are many kinds of deep-seated psychological responses that have been wired into us through evolution and a whole range of things. And some of them really make communicating about climate change difficult. But human beings have always been telling stories to create connection: to reinforce community, common bonds, a sense of obligation and a sense of empathy. Storytelling is so deeply rooted in the way that humans are, that it has to be part of the solution for climate.

Call to action: In this decade that counts, we need women connecting with other women, showing the way through our stories and storytelling. Women sharing our authentic climate stories, our truths to power, our solutions and tips, our strengths and weaknesses, our challenges, our wins and rewards as well as our fears and anxieties.

Here's a checklist to help you get started:

- Can you describe the moment you became engaged with the climate challenge?
- Was there an action you took that led you to another?

- Have you influenced anyone in your family, or friendship group, or workplace, or community and networks?
- How does it feel when you are walking through a forest or feeling the sand between your toes?
- Is there an 'I get it' moment in your life? Maybe it was a tomato you grew at home. Or a supermarket that you influenced by rejecting throwaway plastics and overpackaging? Or a book you read, or film you watched, or podcast you listened to.
- Can you describe what looking after the Earth means to you?

Whatever your climate story is, tell it to others, because you will resonate with someone. You only need your story and an audience of one.

7

CONNECT WITH COUNTRY

By far the most profound learning experience I've had in all the years since I truly began my own climate action journey is gaining more understanding of First Nations peoples and their cultures. Their deeply embedded connection to the land, the water, the skies and all the living things around them underpins authentic storytelling that has been shaped by millennia of living with Mother Earth. Now, in our critical decade, we need to learn from them. Fast.

I see a beautiful and compelling power in how Indigenous peoples connect to the Earth, or to Country, as Aboriginal and Torres Strait Islander people characterise it. A living history of Aboriginal peoples in Australia stretches back across 60,000 years or more.

The most beautiful thing of all that I've experienced first-hand from my Aboriginal and Torres Strait Islander friends and teachers, is being invited to share their knowledge of and relationship with Country. It's incredible cultural generosity, coming from peoples whose traditional lands were seized violently by European settlers two centuries ago. It should inspire us to both embrace the opportunity and show similar generosity ourselves to other people, and peoples, who we can help to lift up.

Like most non-Indigenous Australians of my generation, who went to school in the 1960s and 1970s, I finished my formal education without ever learning much at all about Aboriginal and Torres Strait peoples and their richly diverse cultures, law and lore, spirituality, heritage and mythology.

This reflects Australia's terrible 'white secret', wherein colonisers created the fiction of the Australian continent as 'terra nullius', overrunning the oldest living culture on the planet and declaring it a land without people.

Successive Australian governments sought a 'White Australia' through assimilation policies and practices. After many complex fights for justice and equality, the beginning of constitutional change came via a national referendum in 1967, land rights legislation in the 1970s and 1980s, and the High

Court's dramatic recognition in the 1990s of 'native title' still surviving on some Crown lands.

These changes finally restored a small measure of justice, custodianship and ownership. Even today Aboriginal and Torres Strait Islanders are still struggling to cast aside the destructive legacy of their dispossession once and forever.

Similar scenarios apply for First Nations peoples in other parts of the world too, including the Americas: from the Amazon forests, besieged by land clearing for farming and grazing, to Alaska and its increasingly imperilled permafrost zone, the Arctic tundra.

If we are to fix the climate crisis, and live sustainably on Earth, we have to fix this, too. In Australia, we have to embrace the mantra 'Always was, always is, always will be Aboriginal land'. And the same goes on other continents with other First Nations peoples. It is not enough to simply right past wrongs, which is an ethical imperative; First Nations peoples' amazing reservoir of knowledge for living in balance with Planet Earth must also be highlighted and honoured.

Listen deeply

There is so much the world must urgently learn from First Nations peoples' wisdom: through the legacy of their ancestors, through the generosity of today's generations of

Indigenous peoples, and from the spirituality pulling the past and the future into the now.

It's not for me to tell the story from an Indigenous perspective; my role here is to listen and to share. But I can tell you my story of how I came to discover the beauty of a connection to Country, a mutual connection between land and self.

In my own story, it translates to loving Mother Earth, and forming a respectful and appreciative relationship with her. When you understand the Earth as a living system, it makes you rethink how you live, and the footprints you leave behind you. And once you have this knowledge, you inevitably start thinking very differently about protecting the planet, and the government policies, intervention strategies and social norms that we need to really achieve this.

Recently, in the face of catastrophic bushfires propelled by climate change-driven heat extremes, we've seen communities and institutions learning to adopt Indigenous knowledge of fire management in the Australian natural environment. This includes cool burning techniques, also known as cultural burning, which precede the main bushfire seasons, and use slow-moving ground-level fires that reduce permanent damage to vegetation and make it much easier for wildlife to escape the flames.[43]

In their own storytelling, First Nations peoples are the first scientists, the first farmers, the first people to manage the land.

The entire world needs to bring First Nations knowledge of land management and place-based governance into the way we deal with climate change. Alongside Indigenous law and lore, we also need to understand that nature has rights, and we need to bring that into laws which uphold Country – providing trees, rivers, places and species with similar legal protections to the ones we currently apply to people and property.

We need the voices and wisdom of Indigenous women around every negotiating table. As First Nations peoples teach us, we can only exist in long-term reciprocity with the Earth, not by subjugating and owning it. This means it's important to be honest with ourselves, and to know exactly what we are dealing with in the climate crisis – even if it's hard, really hard, to confront the stark reality of the truth.

But it's really only at this point, staring into the face of a crisis, when we can understand what's at stake for humanity. It's here, right in our hearts, where we'll find the determination to jettison the failed ways and build afresh, which paradoxically includes bringing back ancient wisdoms. We can't just dip our toes in the waters of change, or paddle around a bit, while continuing with our normal way of life. We need to jump in. Boots and all. Together.

We need to adopt and internalise a core belief of First Nations peoples that humans don't own the planet or nature, building our own stories to embed this in our reality. Humans are the caretakers of Country, not the owners, and we have to do a better job of it, because Mother Earth needs us now.

Connecting people and place

Caroline Pidcock is one of Australia's leading sustainability architects, the Chair of the 1 Million Women Board, and my friend. She shared an experience she had in New Zealand while attending a workshop at Otago University in Dunedin on the South Island to study biophilic design, which is the practice of connecting people and nature within our built environments and communities. Caroline recalls:

The Maori people introduce themselves by way of what their mountain is, what their river is, who their family is, and then who they are, because it's a deep acknowledgement of how those places and those people have shaped them. You can dismiss this as not important. But it's an essential realisation of what we really need to come home to and understand.

Rather than defining ourselves by the school we went to, the profession we are part of, or the job we are doing, this begins to help us recognise how important the natural world and the people we surround ourselves with are in shaping who we are. In acknowledging that, you realise a whole lot about yourself.

When I asked Caroline how this realisation had changed her in a practical sense, she told me:

> For the first time in my life, I suddenly appreciated how important the places I grew up in have been in shaping me. I was born in Grafton, on the banks of the mighty Clarence River in the land of the Gumbaynggirr Nation, and then I came to Sydney when I was three and was raised around Sydney Harbour, in the waters and bushlands of the Eora Nation. Those places and waters have been so important to me. And it's a really interesting thing to acknowledge that, not just say it. I now understand that when I need sustenance, or restoration, I go to those landscapes and they make me feel good.

Another non-Indigenous friend, agricultural scientist Anika Molesworth – author of *Our Sunburnt Country*,[44] which is her storytelling of how we can protect our land, our food and our future in the time of global heating – has shared with me how she came to recognise climate change through her relationship with the land and nature on her family's farm in south-western New South Wales. Anika's story includes helping to found Farmers for Climate Action in Australia, now a national network covering over 6000 farms and 35,000 supporters. In her storytelling, Anika recalls:

I've always been an outdoorsy kid. But when we purchased the farm, when I was 12 years old, it felt like I really got it. I fell in love with a place with endless horizons, with the emus marching across the landscape and all this beauty of the natural world. I connected with that.

We purchased the farm in the year 2000, which was the start of the decade-long Millennium Drought. And so those first 10 years I was falling in love with the place and then watching it degrade and being damaged in front of my eyes. I remember the first trips out to the farm here in Broken Hill, with just the awe and wonder of walking around, creeping around the dams and seeing the ducks hiding among the reeds. Seeing joeys pop out of their mother's pouch. And over the seasons and over the years, all of that stuff just gradually disappeared. The animals left. The trees were silent. There were no more birds. The dust storm started rolling in.

And I guess at that point, I didn't quite grasp the climate change concept or I hadn't learned about it yet. But it was this growing sense of worry and the uncertainty of what was going on. Why was all this magic disappearing?

My emerging understanding of First Nations peoples and their cultures has challenged me to better understand the Country where I live. When I moved to Newport on Sydney's upper Northern Beaches early in the 1990s, I knew nothing about the area's Indigenous history. Even now, three decades later, I still have so much to learn. The First Nations peoples living around the Sydney region, as it's now known, were at the frontline when the First Fleet arrived in 1788 to establish a British penal settlement in what became the colony, and now the state of New South Wales.

They bore the brunt of dispossession from their lands, although they never ceded them to the invading settlers. They were among the first to be decimated by smallpox and other diseases brought to virgin shores by the uninvited visitors in their tall ships.

My immediate area on Sydney's Northern Beaches, where this book was written, is the land of the Garigal clan, and I pay my respects to their Elders past, present and future. They are part of the wider Guringai/Wannugine language group.

When I was first drawn to Newport decades ago as a Queenslander relocating to New South Wales, it was an abundance of green open spaces, spectacular beaches and sparkling waterways which attracted me to my new Country. How must this place have felt for the Garigals' ancestors? What incredible knowledge did they accumulate, across many thousands of years, for how to live sustainably from these lands and waterways?

In recent years, I've had the wonderful privilege of finding a new teacher, Aboriginal Elder Aunty Bea Ballangarry. I have learned from her deep insights and mentoring, and her inherent love for Mother Earth, or Miimi Wajaarr in the language of her Gumbaynggirr Nation. I am indebted to Aunty Bea, who is now my dear friend, for guiding me in my journey and for her generosity and pure love.

I am learning more and more from the Indigenous peoples I have the privilege of meeting across Australia and around the world. And in stark contrast to the silence of my school days, I love hearing my eldest granddaughter, Harper, singing about living on Gadigal land thanks to the teachers at her early childhood learning centre.

There's so much to learn from First Nations peoples, but we have to do more, too. We have to emulate their understanding of Country, their deep spiritual connection to Mother Earth, where the land, the rivers and waterways, and the seas are all living systems. We must connect to Country as a living system, and we must appreciate that living systems like islands and rivers have memory and rights.

This is the deepest gift of knowledge our Indigenous communities can share with non-Indigenous peoples across this planet. The message of this accumulated storytelling passed down through millennia is clear: all life is connected, us included.

I am also learning from the wisdom of Dr Anne Poelina, a Nyikina Warrwa woman who belongs to the Mardoowarra people, from the lower Fitzroy River area in the Kimberley region of Western Australia.

Anne says: 'I am a woman who belongs to the Fitzroy River. Not in terms of property rights, but a law of obligation to protect the river's right to live and to flow.'

Reflecting the cultural generosity of First Nations peoples, she invites non-Indigenous peoples in:

Come sit on the riverbanks with us. This nation belongs to us all and we must be a coalition of hope. We want to teach people how to live with the land. The Country is alive. We can't do anything without including Country. So get to know Indigenous peoples.

Sixty per cent of non-Indigenous people still haven't met an Aboriginal person. That must change. But also I am asking you to find your own riverbank and your own story with Country. Country is Country, and Country wants you to know. We can show you how to feel and hear Country. When you heal Country, you heal us all. It is a gift to be a human being to see with our ears and to listen with our eyes. And that's what our Elders have told us.

Protecting Country together

As a traditional custodian of the Kimberley region, Anne is fighting for the rights of the Fitzroy River as a sacred ancestral being. Right now the Kimberley and its peoples are under threat from ever-expanding industrialisation linked to mining, pastoralism and agriculture. It's a remote place, blessed with ecological diversity, and is home to about 200 Aboriginal communities representing the oldest living culture on the planet.

This is an excerpt from Anne's talk at the Women's Climate Congress, 2021:

The rivers are living systems. They hold Memory. We have to recognise the property rights rivers have. Rivers have a right to flow, and it is time to stop unjust development. The Fitzroy River is National Heritage. It is the largest registered Aboriginal cultural heritage site in Western Australia. The battle will be won through grassroots organisations, Indigenous and non-Indigenous together.

As Indigenous people, we are given a totem, an animal creature that we have bonded to for life. My totem is the blue tongue lizard. So what that does, is, it teaches us that governance needs to be flat. It needs to be horizontal rather than hierarchical. We're saying that even factoring in the wellbeing, we need to think about a non-human family as well because they teach us to be fully human.

So for me, it's not so much about gender issues of male versus female. Really, at the end of the day, what we're talking about is values and ethics and how we bring that into framing what good governance could look like, what it must look like. And so from Aboriginal people, we lived with this land. We were the first everything, all of the first scientists, the first engineers, the first astronomers, the first architects. And we came from a world where we always saw ourselves, as belonging to a world of 'we, not me'.

Her way of describing First Nations law, culture, governance structure and care of Country is something each and every one of us needs to hear.

Anne's poem, 'First Law: Matrix or Patrix', is an exquisite homage to Mother Earth and to the challenge we all face and must rise to in reshaping our current world. Her poem begins:

Deconstructing the Patrix is not about confusing the Matrix
What has COVID19 taught us as human beings?
Where has the greed of the predatory elite taken us
Can we pause and take a deeper breath?
Can we Dream ... new Dreams, in this modern Dreamtime?

Nyikina Warrwa

Yimardoowarra Marnin

Anne Poelina Wagaba

I'm also learning from my beautiful young friend, Tish King, proud Zenadth Kes/Torres Strait Island woman with strong connections to Masig Island and Badu Island. Her communities are on the frontline of climate change here in Australia, and Tish is stepping into her agency as a powerful young woman fighting for her beloved lands and peoples.

Working for Seed Mob, Australia's first Indigenous youth climate network, Tish also was at COP26 in Glasgow, as a voice for our First Nations peoples. I love our conversations.

When chatting with her for this book, I was telling Tish about my trip to the Micronesian Women's Conference in 2017, hosted by the Marshall Islands. While there I witnessed first-hand the ravages of climate change from sea level rise, and I heard the stories from women across the Pacific: Fiji, Kiribati, Nauru, Palau, Solomon Islands, Tonga, Tuvalu and Vanuatu, as well as the Marshall Islands.

The stories of sea level rise were deeply moving, yet I hadn't connected it to what was happening in my own country's Torres Strait communities – Tish's Country.

The Torres Strait is Australia's northernmost frontier, stretching from the tip of Queensland to the southern shores of Papua New Guinea. Communities there are experiencing exactly the same frontline climate issues as Pacific Islanders, including inundation by the sea. In a response, women like Tish are bringing their stories front and centre.

When we spoke, Tish hadn't been home to her beloved Torres Strait for a long time, spending most of her time on the mainland. She was sharing her story with me about what it felt like going back.

I'm a proud Kulkalaig woman, of Kulkalgal Nation from the island of Masig. I come from really strong blood families that have been resisting and educating for as long as I can remember. Hearing all the old stories from my Elders and their incredible strength and resilience through a time that was so shifting just empowers me to want to do the same.

Those stories are built into our lands, which are built into us. For me, as a proud Torres Strait Islander woman, my stories are through the stars and the sea ...

I have already seen first-hand the impacts of the climate crisis on my island home, Masig. Where the summer of 2020 and 2021, I picked up the bones of my matriarch, whose burial ground had been desecrated from sea levels rising. I felt hurt. I felt I had disrespected my old people.

It was a reminder that those who contribute the least to climate change are often the most impacted. I saw the erosion, the sea level rise, and how global warming has exacerbated weather events like monsoons and king tides.

The fish have left our coral seas, and when we can't fish, we can't practice culture. The dugongs have left because the seagrass is dying. Our totems and ancestors are leaving us, and our food security hangs in the balance.

I'm scared about what will happen to my old people. Effective environmental policy is required and First Nations people must have a seat at the table. It must be place-based, deliberative and culturally safe.

Thinking about Dr Anne Poelina's invitation to come sit on a riverbank with First Nations peoples and learn how to listen to Country, I asked Tish to describe what she would say to me on that riverbank, or at least her version of it:

Okay Nat, let's instead take this to the beach. The first thing you do is, naturally, you take off your shoes. For me personally it's because I want to feel my skin to be connected to the ground and feel that electricity. I feel connected to country and I feel grounded. It lights me up.

Then sit down and take in big, deep breaths and appreciate where we are. Inhale this goodness and exhale whatever we were feeling before we got here, because we naturally will be thinking about something, carrying something. And then I would just sit in silence. Really take in and reflect what's around you.

What are the sounds that you can hear? Close your eyes. Using all your senses. What do you smell? What can you taste? And then I'd share a story. Just naturally. Something of me to share with you. Like, even how you wanted me to take you to a riverbank? We all appreciate being in nature. Why? Because being outside in nature has healing powers, it has our stories, our songs and our history. That's a really good reason why we're protecting it.

Opening the Circle

During COVID-19, the 1 Million Women team hosted our second LoveEarth Festival online with 650 women from across the globe, with thousands more watching on Facebook. And the storytelling flowed so wonderfully in those two hours.

There was Aunty Bea connecting us all to Country and musical performances from Missy Higgins, Paul Kelly, Alice Skye and Uncle Kev Carmody. A big dose of stubborn optimism from Christiana Figueres. A rallying call to women from Mary Robinson asking us all to not just imagine a new world, but to live it, now. There was climate psychology and poetry and conversation on how to 'live' climate action.

We laughed and cried and sang and listened. It was utterly joyful that we were all together as a community of women from across the Earth, albeit virtually, after a terrible year of navigating the pandemic and ongoing climate catastrophes.

And it was deeply moving, made so by all the connections to Country and place which came through every piece of storytelling.

Celebrated Australian singer-songwriter Missy Higgins shared her life-changing story of going to Broome in the Kimberley region, where she lived for an extended period of time. The connection she formed with the land is something she'd never experienced before:

> The land was alive and in charge. It was so full of energy and so powerful and sometimes humans get the feeling we are the ones in charge. Being in Broome was the most grounded I have felt. It's more important than ever to feel the wilderness and the bush.

Opening our online event – and at the very heart of it – was Aunty Bea's Circle. This is how Aunty Bea explains the Circle Work she leads:

> I believe that holding Circles put all of us on the same level. We're all looking at each other on the same level, and there's no linear image. When we sit in this way we think differently. I also believe we think differently when we're sitting than when we're standing. It's grounding. People listen to each other. When we are sitting, it's a

collective, it's a family, it's a mob. I'm so strong when I'm on the same level. Where nobody talks over the other person.

When the person is holding the stone, they are speaking. Circle work is listening. We get to listen to each other. In my way of thinking, we get to listen more than we talk, and then it gives a chance for everybody to speak, and it gives a chance for everybody to listen. That's my total commitment towards the way forward.

And if we can get people to come to the place where the entire universe is not separate, every part of it – our trees, animals and birds, our systems, our Miimi Wajaarr, our Mother Earth – are part of the whole then we can move forward.

We're not separate. That's the way that Indigenous folk – and I'm talking again from my growing up, my perspective, saw it – we are all part of the whole. We're all part of the system. If I ache, then I'm sure somewhere out there, the trees in my front yard or the front lawn, are aching too.

First Nations peoples offer us even more than their wisdom, cultural understanding and experience of living lightly on the planet. Their story – so often with women stepping up – is inspirational. It speaks to courage, incredible resilience,

Listen through the soles of your feet, through the textures and aromas of the air around you, through the sounds of nature.

determination, asserting their truths to power, and the depth, sincerity and authenticity of their storytelling.

Call to action: Get connected with Country. Sit on a riverbank as Dr Anne Poelina invites us to, or a beach as Tish King suggests, and reflect. Listen to Mother Earth, to Aunty Bea's Miimi Wajaarr. Listen to the very heartbeat of the planet, to the trees, the wind, the ocean, the rivers and all the elements – and deeply hear what is being 'said'. Listen through the soles of your feet, through the textures and aromas of the air around you, through the sounds of nature. Stop, connect and listen with intent, and know what an extraordinary Earth we are part of.

8

A FAREWELL TO CONSUMERISM

In this defining decade for climate action, we have to put ourselves on a very different path. A path where we won't define ourselves by what we consume, but instead by what we contribute and add-back as conscious citizens of this planet.

Women dominate consumer purchasing for our households, with estimates of their average 'share of the shopping' typically ranging from 70 per cent upwards. This gives us the opportunity to make our money speak.

A *Forbes* article, *20 Facts and Figures to Know When Marketing to Women*, stresses women's brand loyalty as a key facet of our market influence, with 85 per cent of women saying they will stay loyal to brands they like.[45]

Nothing speaks more clearly to brands and businesses than our willingness to buy their products and services, or to reject them. Whether we spend our money on something, or don't, is powerful storytelling in its own right. How we behave as consumers is also the basis of a climate action agenda which we can mobilise right now, today, and which we can follow every day of our lives.

We need to reform ourselves and redeem consumerism. Or get a new word altogether, one that speaks to circularity and interconnectedness, not fast turnaround exploitation followed by landfill. Maybe that's it: reshape consumption as 'circularism', and consumers as 'circularists'.

I found an article in the online magazine *Grist* tracking the origins and meaning of 'consumerism', saying: 'The roots of *consumer* offer the first hints of trouble. It traces back to the Latin *consumere*, meaning to destroy, devour, waste, or squander. From there, it's only a slight leap to today's definition: "a person who uses up a commodity; a purchaser of goods or services," according to the Oxford English Dictionary.'[46]

Consumerism is a multi-layered and complex issue and it isn't equal. Wealth isn't equal. Those who hold much of the world's wealth just happen to be those who have benefited most from fossil fuels, with the greatest responsibility for our climate crisis.

Those who hold much of the world's wealth just happen to be those who have benefited most from fossil fuels, with the greatest responsibility for our climate crisis.

For each of us, the bottom line is that we need to buy less – much less. But consumerism runs much deeper than this. What it's really about is going down this path of understanding, in our core, that happiness is not about consuming.

I think in an affluent society we often fall into the trap of really believing this: that happiness is about consuming, the more the better. We really believe the more we have, the happier we will be. And it just doesn't work that way.

There is a spiritual dimension to redeeming our consumerism. I can imagine a mantra: 'my happiness and contentment are not driven by the stuff I consume.'

We need to find our spiritual connection with our Earth, and to a deep love of nature. We need to know in our hearts that this is what matters. The many miracles of life on Earth.

The wisdom our First Nations people teach us. A walk in a forest. Gazing out to sea from a golden beach. Morning dew on a spider's web, glistening in the early sunlight. It really is all connected, and we have to connect with it and feel the wonder.

We need to embrace a state of mind where purpose and recognition of unintended costs and harmful consequences frame the purchasing decisions we make. Where we automatically reuse things, extend their useful lives with repairs and pre-used sharing, and recycle for their next life. So understanding that all the stuff we buy never disappears and appreciating the embedded carbon that went into making the product in the first place helps us hold onto things as long as we can.

We need a world where manufacturers operate in a circular economy, designing *out* waste and harmful impacts, and designing *in* restoration and regeneration. A world where we take sustained pride and delight in what we save and recirculate, rather than seeking fleeting joy in flashy new things we will soon discard for the next thing.

An Oxfam report from 2020 reported in *The Guardian* highlights the real cost of wastefully extravagant lifestyles: if left unchecked, in the next decade the carbon emissions of the world's richest 10 per cent would be enough to raise greenhouse gas pollution levels in the atmosphere above the point likely to increase temperatures by 1.5°C ... even if the whole of the rest of the world cut their emissions to zero immediately.[47]

We need to embrace a state of mind where purpose and recognition of unintended costs and harmful consequences frame the purchasing decisions we make.

Consumerism isn't sustainable

Indian-born Professor Veena Sahajwalla brings an industrial perspective to this, helping me to understand it better as an everyday consumer.

An amazing woman, highly recognised in academic and public circles, Veena has been a 1 Million Women ambassador since the beginning. She and her engineering team at the University of New South Wales in Sydney turn textile and glass waste – normally destined for landfill – into fire- and water-resistant building materials.

Veena sees waste as an opportunity to explore, rather than a problem to be managed. Having grown up in Mumbai, India, she recalls rubbish heaps there being trawled by hand for plastic, cardboard and other materials of value to sell on to scrap dealers.

'The sense of repurposing and reusing and sharing was driven by economic necessity, of course, but people were more than happy to have hand-me-downs, whether it was clothes or furniture items,' says Veena. 'We would rarely throw away things that were in decent working order.'

This attitude used to be prevalent in the West, especially for the generation which survived the Great Depression. But since the postwar economic boom of the fifties, we've created a warped, wasteful, unthinking kind of mass consumerism. This has become such a deeply embedded part of our psyche. Almost from the day we are born advertisers are bombarding us as we grow up: 'Look like this. Be like this. Buy this.'

It just hits you from an incredibly early age, before you can know any better. This means it's hard work not to be complicit, through ignorance or apathy, if not intent. We need to take ourselves out of the structured framework of our high consumption society. And that's not easy. But every time we don't succumb to the marketing hype, every time we reject the siren's call that 'we can only be happy when we are consuming', then we are carving out that new path.

I'm not naive about the massive cultural change being canvassed here, and the enormous challenge we face as human society to change course. Consumerism is the commercial backbone of market-based democratic societies like Australia, where I live, and is a powerful societal force in many non-democratic ones as well.

In many ways, people equate consumer choice to freedom itself, and governments interpret high and rising levels of consumption as evidence of successful economies. So mess with it at your peril.

My time on the dark side

I have my own past on the consumerism dark side. Before I started 1 Million Women, I ran my own cosmetics business for 24 years. I lived a very different life from the one I live now. It was all about overpackaging, microbeads, shimmers and glitters. I was part of the fast fashion industry, churning out products I wanted you to buy.

This wasn't how I started off, however. In the early days of my manufacturing career I created a beautiful brand with a holistic approach, one which reflected my values. I used minimal package, and no preservatives; it was cruelty free and based on goodness, relaxation and natural ingredients such as plant extracts. I'd travel around Australia, and internationally, evangelising for my products and my philosophy.

I would tell anyone I could that true beauty comes from within. My message was it really didn't matter if you bought my skincare product (or anyone else's for that matter), it simply wouldn't work if you didn't marry it up with inner health and wellbeing. That how we look is a mirror of how we feel. I made a point of stressing that to be honestly and purely beautiful it needs to come from within, and skincare products are not the elixir of eternal youth. Health and wellbeing are the foundations to pure beauty.

I loved that brand so much. I believed deeply in the message I was selling. It was an honest story about skincare in an industry that makes you feel you can't possibly be beautiful unless you use 15 different products for your skin. (Just for the record, you really only need one or two. Well, that's all I use anyway: a moisturising oil for my skin and a sunscreen.) But the message I was selling was off-base for a mass consumer marketplace.

Commercial reality caught up with me and my fledgling cosmetics business. I saw opportunities to grow my business by targeting the big national chain stores in Australia and internationally.

In this commercially turbocharged world, every brand is competing for the best shelf space. Brands that can afford it pay for the best high traffic space in the shop. Every brand is compelled to launch an endless stream of new products to push its competitor off the shelf, and to keep the marketing machine going. It was an exhausting business, trying to keep up year after year, and both the competition and retail outlet demands were relentless.

In this commercially turbocharged world, every brand is competing for the best shelf space.

Decades later, I see nothing has slowed down. The cosmetics industry today turns over in excess of $US511 billion annually (2021).[48] According to recent beauty industry statistics, not even a weak economy can hold this industry back. It is predicted to exceed \$US716 billion by 2025.[49] You need look no further for proof of marketing triumphing over reality.

So in my quest to grow as a small business owner, I'd been seduced by department store chains and the fast fashion industry. I was asked to manufacture Christmas lines for just about every department store chain in Australia, and I can tell you I was ridiculously excited at the time. Creating fast-fashion Christmas brands for department stores is potentially a huge money-making business, and I was hooked.

For me, the conflicts piled up faster than I could cope, and my values were sacrificed. On one hand, I was still manufacturing my beautiful, very boutique 'true beauty comes from within' honest brand, with minimal everything – including sales. On the other hand, I quickly became a fast-growing player in perpetuating consumerism with fast fashion crap. I justified doing one to support the other.

As this side of the business took off, the only thing I became concerned about was how quickly my products in the department stores sold. Not the quality of the product and not the longevity of the product – just if it jumped off the shelf and into your trolley and through the checkout. I knew when you bought my products they would probably end up in the bin quickly. I was numb to that. I was too busy selling you cheap products fast, exhilarated at the speed at which you took them home.

Manufacturers of consumer goods want you to believe you are a consumer first, and that your consumerism defines who you are and shapes your personality. I contributed to this whole engine of marketing, making you believe you needed my product to be happy.

The fast fashion brands I created were the perfect recipe for the quick sale. Tween girls were my target market. I sold them the dream: that if they wore my swizzle-sparkled, triple-coloured lip gloss and whatever else was in the pack, they'd stand out in the crowd. The packs sold like hot cakes. Who wouldn't want one? They were bursting with colour and fun, and at $9.99 they were sold at a magic price point for spontaneous purchases.

That's all a long time ago now, before I got the point about climate change. I eventually stopped being a cosmetics manufacturer to start 1 Million Women. My learnings from my manufacturing and marketing days came with me too. I understand the psyche of the consumer.

I was in the business of selling you happiness, and every time you purchased my products you validated that what I was doing was right. Instead, if you had left my product on the shelf, it would have sent a message directly back to me that you didn't want it. The store buyers would have got the message as well, and that may have ended my time on their shelves. It would have made them, and me, think differently.

Turning the tide on wastefulness

When I think about my original brand, the one with the 'honest' skincare story, I realise how much of its philosophy feeds into my 1 Million Women thinking. True beauty comes from within. Looking after ourselves from the inside is a microcosm of our bigger picture. The macro equivalent is Mother Earth, and every species living on her. Every single thing is interconnected and looking after the Earth can't be skin-deep.

Not so long ago I heard a politician, yet another bloke, on the radio telling people how we need to get out there and spend, spend, spend. He was saying, with no hint of wider awareness, that consumers are needed to feed economic growth.

What more evidence do governments need to change this message? We need an economy for people and our planet, not a bigger one at any cost. When I mentioned this on social media on 1 Million Women's Instagram, one of our community members responded: 'Economies need to flow, not grow. Wanting bigger profit growth every year is unsustainable and absurd greed.'

I love that description. Economies need to flow, not grow. We can't have limitless consumption on a planet which has limited resources. To be sustainable, we need a completely different approach.

We need to reset our world this decade: decoupling economic growth from environmental destruction, replacing exploitation with regeneration, moving from our throwaway culture to reusing and conserving resources wherever we can, and embracing renewable energy to power the world.

Capitalism, consumerism and climate change are all linked. I am not an economist, but it seems so obvious to the layperson: the model is broken! Overconsumption is all wrapped up in capitalism running riot. The transformation we need now, however, means the complete opposite is required. Capitalism is such a human construct, especially when its success or otherwise is measured in how much we produce and consume, rather than what we destroy to do it. It doesn't have the rights of nature embedded in it. It doesn't support climate justice. It just pushes this dangerously illogical approach of needing to spend at all costs, and keep growing.

Nicki Hutley is our 1 Million Women economic adviser and my great friend. She's a highly experienced economist, having spent more than three decades working in the financial and investment markets and in economic consulting. So I asked for her take on finding economic 'flow' that doesn't replicate the ethos of economic growth at any cost. Nicki puts it this way:

Economic growth is good, in theory at least, because as we raise living standards for the average, we have more resources to help those who are most in need. And so, if we let living standards decline, those who are most vulnerable will be most affected.

So the real question, according to Nicki, is how do you have 'good growth'? And what does good growth look like anyway? And, as Nicki paints it, governments can reset economic policies for good growth by legislating for sustainability:

> Growth that understands your impact on the environment and your impact across society is good growth. We economists call that looking at the externalities. So if we take coal-fired power stations, for example, you pay for your electricity. But we don't pay for the emissions that are going into the atmosphere. And good economics says we should all pay for that. We need to price those externalities when we do things.
>
> That will send the right price signal to say we know that for every additional tonne of carbon dioxide in the atmosphere, we are creating a problem which has a cost. At the moment, in Australia and in many places around the world, we don't pay a price for that. Unfortunately, we should. And then it would help people to make better decisions, and help firms by encouraging them to produce better products.

For Nicki, capitalism and consumerism can be redirected away from the bad, towards the good:

> As an individual consumer, you can think about these externalities too. We might not have a spreadsheet and go through all of the Excel calculations, but we can say, 'there's two products on the shelf and this one appears to be a little bit cheaper, but it's made overseas, so it's going to have a higher carbon footprint from transport.' It might be made in a market with modern slavery involved. Or this one is non-recyclable, whereas this one can go into the compost.

As you can see, there are all these things we can think about as conscious consumers, and also as politicians and policymakers, and which we can act on too. Number one is putting a dollar price on carbon pollution, to guide purchasing and investment decisions away from the bad and towards the good. Nicki explains the real-world value of 'price signals' for accelerating climate action:

> We shouldn't fuel economic growth for economic growth's sake. It's not just the cost of the product. It's what it is doing to the environment. People get a bit narky about economics and economists, but there are some

very basic truths that say that price signals work and a carbon price sends the strongest possible signal that you can to the market to say, 'this is the most sensible way you can accelerate the change because we have basically run out of time.'

Talking to Nicki is one of my favourite things. We have been chatting about the economics of climate change, and the social and environmental impacts of our choices, for many years now. Her point about bringing the externalities into our purchasing decisions is key.

Fast fashion has hidden costs. So do the food we eat, the vehicles we drive, and the houses we live in. Putting a price on carbon pollution is an economist's recipe for fixing the problem of one externality that isn't being accounted for. And depending on what they want to encourage or discourage, governments can use taxes and subsidies to adjust pricing, and as voters we need to pay close attention. From a climate action perspective, we applaud rebates to make clean technology solutions like solar panels and electric vehicles more affordable, but we deplore subsidies to make fossil fuels cheaper.

As citizens of the planet, we need to understand the 'true value' of things we buy, including all the externalities, and pay accordingly. But it's not the only thing we can do.

This idea of economies flowing is such a beautiful one. It's circular in design, which is completely opposite to our current linear approach of 'purchase something, use it, then throw it away.' The circular economy represents a shift in the way things are manufactured and valued.

It's actually a reflection of nature, because resources flow within natural ecosystems. Animals breathe in oxygen and breathe out carbon dioxide while plants breathe in carbon dioxide and emit oxygen back into the atmosphere. There's a balance, a natural balance, and people are well advised not to mess with it.

Aside from the miracle of sunlight falling on the Earth as wonderfully accessible energy, people and our planet have to make do with the resources we have. The Earth is a closed system, and it needs care. I love the way 1 Million Women climate adviser Professor Lesley Hughes puts it:

We need to get away from the 'growth is good' mantra of Western democracy, finding a different economic flow that goes round and gives back. And hopefully with less stuff. I think that we need to shift from being a 'buying stuff' based economy to a 'buying experiences and services economy'. Let's stop going to the mall to wander around as entertainment, to just buy stuff. Let's experience more nature and spend our money on doing things rather than acquiring things.

Over my years with 1 Million Women I have witnessed an avalanche of manufacturers and brands embracing that flow of the circular economy with zero waste, zero packaging, sustainable manufacturing processes and carbon neutral supply chains. None of this was *ever* in the conversation when I was a cosmetics manufacturer. It never entered my head, nor the heads of any of the suppliers I was dealing with, nor the store buyers' heads either. Waste was just waste. A product had just one shelf life before it found its way into landfill.

Take plastic pollution, for example. Based on a McKinsey sustainability report, if plastics demand follows its current trajectory, global plastics waste volume will grow from 260 million tons per year in 2016 to 460 million by 2030.[50]

Or clothes. In 1930, the average American woman owned nine outfits. Today, that figure is 30 outfits – one for every day of the month.[51] Globally, an estimated 92 million tonnes of textile waste is created each year, the equivalent to a rubbish truck full of clothes ending up in landfill every second. By 2030, globally we are expected as a whole to be discarding more than 134 million tonnes of textiles a year.[52]

Reduce, reuse, recycle, reset

Ellen MacArthur, founder of the circular economy thinktank the Ellen MacArthur Foundation in the United Kingdom, sees enormous opportunities in reforming the fashion industry.

'There's a $US500 billion opportunity if we can get this right,' she says. 'If we can keep that fashion cycling for longer, if we can recover that material.'

Material which isn't being recycled represents huge value being lost every day of every year. That's value to the economy, value to the fashion industry, which is being turned into waste and pollution when it could be flowing around in a beneficial life cycle.

I put up a post on 1 Million Women's Instagram page recently. It had this very simple message of 'Let's normalise outfit repeating', shared in an image from the illustrator @sophillustrates.

We added our own message about removing the stigma around wearing the same outfit repeatedly. I couldn't believe the response the image prompted. Over 10,000 likes, 1483 shares, and 200-plus comments. So many of the comments were women saying, I feel guilty when wearing the same clothes.

This article from *peppermint* magazine explains:

Most women from western cultures are familiar with the metaphorical stain outfit-repeating can leave on our garments, even if it's simply yelling into a heaving closet, "I have nothing to wear!" If not personally, perhaps they've seen the press call out female celebrities for re-wearing their threads. That our society considers outfit-repeating newsworthy signals the value placed on a woman's appearance.[53]

The article goes on to say that embracing outfit-repeating will not only help reduce the stigma caused by sexism, consumerism and classism, it will also reduce our carbon footprint.

So we need to unburden and 'unguilt' ourselves. We need to treasure the flow more than the stuff. Every time we resist societal pressure to never age, to look like an Instagram influencer, to have a different outfit for every day of the month, we're helping the planet and future generations. We're also paving the way for others to feel okay about wearing the same outfit multiple times. We need to work together to reset society's expectations and relieve the pressure on people, and on women especially, to conform with the tyranny of fast fashion.

We can all play our part in the circular economy. We can buy things with the expectation that we'll have them for a very long time. And if we find we're finished with them, we can share, mend, swap, give or upcycle, using our own skills or the skills of the community.

Of course there's more to it than this. We have to boycott products which are inherently wasteful and polluting, like single-use plastics and throw-away fast fashion. When we vote in the marketplace, with our dollars, it's vital not to support carbon-intensive products perpetuating the climate crisis.

For example, you can choose to power your home with renewable energy, buy local and sustainably grown produce, and look out for non-plastic and minimal packaging. Taking efficient public transport is a good alternative to putting petrol in the car.

When we do this, investing our money even in a simple purchase, we also need to think about externalities: like carbon pollution going up into the atmosphere, plastics ending up in the oceans, species being pushed to extinction, and the unsafe workplaces many consumer brands employ.

On this, I believe women will lead the way. It's estimated that women now control nearly one-third (32 per cent) of the world's wealth,[54] and that by 2028 women will be responsible for up to three-quarters of consumer spending worldwide.[55] Women are far more likely than men to be responsible for household spending.

On average, 89 per cent of women across the world report either controlling or sharing daily shopping needs, compared with only 41 per cent of men.[56] Women not only have the buying power, they have the influence. As the majority of primary caregivers for children and the elderly, women spend significant time and money buying on behalf of others. Women are the gateway to the people in their households, as well as in their social and business networks.

Beyond divesting from harmful practices, we can use our spending to actively support others. Putting our money towards businesses with social and environmental missions can pave the way for positive growth. We can choose to support local business, women-run business and First Nations brands, and feel empowered when we buy something, knowing our dollar is lifting someone up instead of tearing the planet down.

Putting our money towards businesses with social and environmental missions can pave the way for positive growth.

We can really value each dollar, and the journey that each dollar takes – making economic flow the height of fashionable living.

Lorena Aguilar explains her framework for buying:

I have a purchase decision that is framed by human rights and it's framed by a green approach. I want to purchase products that I know have not violated human rights and they have really looked after the environment. But we need to convince more people, and we need to bring them into this market where they know it's cool. And that's where we need the media and marketing agencies on board. We need to start selling that being green and supporting low-carbon solutions, small and local, is the coolest and smartest thing you can do.

I was always surprised in the early days of 1 Million Women when people would say to me: 'What does it matter how we live?' or 'It's no-one else's business how I want to live my life.' Everything matters!

How we live matters. How we vote matters. The pressure we put on governments, politicians and policy-makers matters. The stance we take against socially and environmentally harmful corporations and abusive brands matters. Collective action matters. Reducing waste matters.

We can't approach looking after the planet as an adjunct to how we live, not in this decade that means so much. We can't on the one hand march in the streets and put pressure on governments, then on the other turn around and live a life filled with overconsumption. We can't say: 'Well I've done my bit over here – by marching in protest, or recycling a bit, or buying an eco brand – so I can do this bad or questionable thing over there.'

To reset our world, we have to change this emotionally within ourselves, as well as at the point of payment. We only have this decade to put ourselves on a different path. A path of conscious decision-making. A path where we actually don't see ourselves as consumers at all. Where we see ourselves as citizens of this planet. Then, with every single thing we do, every dollar we spend or invest, we can vote for the good of the planet and humanity.

> **Call to action:** Cut your 'buying more stuff' consumerism by at least half, starting right now. With every purchase, ask yourself questions like: 'Do I really need this? Could I purchase this locally? Can I buy it second hand? Is there an 'experience' I could substitute?' What are the externalities I need to think about, like how far did it travel to get onto the shelf? Will it last for a really long time and what am I going to do when I'm finished with it?
>
> Learn to cherish and repair and mend the things you already have, and buy sustainably when you really need to.
>
> How to spot greenwashing:
>
> 1. Don't be fooled by environmental imagery – just because it looks earthy doesn't mean it's as good for the planet as it implies.
> 2. Watch out for false and misleading labels. Be wary if there is no supportive information to explain how the product fits the claims.

3. Look out for hidden trade-offs. For example, when a product has recycled packaging but the contents are unsustainable. Like a pack of balloons packaged in recycled materials. Or a fast fashion brand using sustainable or natural materials while the clothing is made in exploitative working conditions.

9

THE SPIRIT OF COMMUNITY

Building community around climate action is fundamental to holding the 1.5°C line in this decade.

At a local level, we must engage to demand more green spaces, better air quality in our neighbourhoods and better transport solutions. It doesn't matter whether that looks like more walkways and cycleways and more bike parking, or improved and inclusive public transit systems, or electrifying our buses; what matters is that within our own communities, we are changing the status quo.

When your community is about place, it's deeply personal.

It's about where you live and the people you see on a daily basis, so when you make a change it's easy to see.

It's about being part of a grassroots community holding a local politician accountable for their shameful climate inaction; or standing up to coal mines, or fracking, or land clearing, or major development.

Or planning and working collectively towards a local community that's sustainable, or 100 per cent renewable for energy, or net zero for greenhouse gas pollution, or all of these things. It could be a community food garden, alternative food networks or a community solar farm; or a community battery for storing and sharing locally generated clean energy.

Our cities and towns, suburbs and regions need to transform in this decade, and the communities within them need to play a huge role in advocating and lobbying for what's needed. In 2018, a gender-inclusive climate action report from C40 Cities stated 54 per cent of the world's population live in cities.[57] While cities account for just 2 per cent of the Earth's surface, 70 per cent of total greenhouse gas emissions are produced by this 2 per cent.

It highlights that to implement the 1.5°C Paris Agreement target in this decade, and achieve the sweeping climate action we need, cities have to include all of their citizens in the solutions. Gender is an important factor that influences peoples' lived experiences within a city, or anywhere for that matter, as well as their vulnerability to climate impacts and their ability to mitigate them.

As we strive to reset our world, we can harness the spirit of community. The strength of community is circular. It's inclusive. Driven by purpose. The moment you step into a community environment, magic can happen. It can bring out the best in you and others around you. There is shared vision, collaboration, joy, highs and lows, and wins and losses, all experienced together.

Being part of a community moves us on from the 'isolated me' trend of modern living – where you may not even know who your neighbours are – to the 'collective we'. It is local to where you live – a street, a suburb, a town.

With climate anxiety on the rise, research shows us that acting in our own community in unison with others helps to address despair and feelings of powerlessness.[58] It helps to keep us determined and optimistic, and nurtures our resilience and resolve. And for our right here right now mission, we have to keep topping up the tank of self-motivation whenever we can.

When you bring the community together, a different conversation unfolds. People are concerned for each other, for the place they live, for equity and fairness. Done well, it's a support network. It helps us step into spaces we may not normally go to because we are supported by others. It helps us find or restore

The strength of community is circular. It's inclusive. Driven by purpose.

our individual agency, while at the same time strengthening our collective agency. It sets us up to be collectively resilient.

It makes us kinder and more compassionate human beings to collectively contribute to an issue or a project. It makes us invest our presence and time into the place we live. When we are part of a community, the 'collective we' has real agency and power to effect change. And that is vital for this decade of climate action. It is critical to resetting our world.

Creating nested systems

Research shows that women of all ages are contributing to their local community, much more so than men, and there's nothing surprising about this at all. Women are more likely to be part of communities. Women are more likely to volunteer.

This extract from 'Civic Nation', a *Forbes* feature, illustrates how women's strong involvement in community is a global phenomenon:

Women are also more likely to be the primary caregivers in their homes, meaning that they spend more time with diverse members of their communities, including teachers and healthcare providers. As a result, women may be more exposed to social injustices and volunteer opportunities in their own communities in comparison to their male-identifying counterparts, providing greater motivation to become civically involved and engaged.[59]

We also have repair work to do on the community front. We've allowed an anti-community element to work its way into modern living, especially in wealthier, westernised cultures. Many Australians, and I suspect people in many countries, often think of our homes as being our 'castles'. We go inside and shut the door, metaphorically raising the drawbridge, to close out the world and everything about it which unsettles us.

Architect and sustainability advocate Caroline Pidcock embraces regenerative and biophilic design when it comes to the places where we live, concepts which are all about restoring nature and bringing the love of Earth into our homes. Not just the structures that put a roof over our heads, but a wider sense of place. How we identify with the land we live on, and how important it is to think about where we live. And how it's connected to the local neighbourhood we live in, and how this cascades out into the wider global community.

Caroline talks about it as 'nested systems'. In a nested system there's you as an individual, and you live in a family as part of a community or neighbourhood, and then a local area, a state, a country, and the world. Each of those circles or rings is connected, and they all interact with one another. So we are always operating at all levels, in varying levels of intensity, at varying times of the days and seasons. Caroline explains:

> I feel modern architecture often disconnects us from 'place', and where we are, with this idea you can come in and build whatever you like, wherever you like, regardless of the nature of this 'place'. Also, we can think about how we integrate and think beyond our room and our house and into the garden and neighbourhood beyond.
>
> We don't have to own anything to have it form an important part of our life. We can look more carefully at the local parks, community centres and libraries – the local places and spaces where you can expand your living into, in meaningful ways by yourself and with your neighbours. Resilience and joy come from the diversity and strength that can be created through these relationships and connections.

We have a collective opportunity to invest in our local communities so that they thrive. It's about being 'present', locally, in a physical sense, in your 'place'. It maps to Country, in its Indigenous cultural sense, when it is genuinely place-based, and it's how people mobilise together to take stands and speak truth to power.

We don't all need to be the leaders of movements. But with what is at stake, and with the rapidly diminishing timeframe we have left to reset our world, starting with staying under 1.5°C of average global temperature rise, we need to join in. When you buy locally, the local community prospers. When your community plants trees, or restores bushland, or cleans up a creek, you can see the benefits with your own eyes.

In recent times, we've seen how bushfires, floods and climate-fuelled extreme weather events have brought communities together in the face of adversity, and in genuine battles for survival. The global pandemic has exposed how critical our support for local communities and local businesses is. I think many of us have re-engaged with our community because of COVID-19. It stripped away a lot of what distracts us from 'local', including travel culture, and reacquainted us with simple joys like taking a walk right where you are.

Participating in your local community with real intent is a lot more than just living in a community. It's about sharing both challenges and opportunities, and contributing to the greater good.

I've always thought I was an engaged citizen of my own local community. The primary school at the bottom of my street, the high school just up the road, and the years of Saturday morning sport were a big focus when our children were young. With kids at high school, I always put my hand up for the musical after-parties. I support the local hairdresser, the local shops, and local restaurants. I love the farmers' market, and the local cinema. I love where I live and have a deep spiritual connection to the land and the beach. Some of my dearest friends live in my community.

It has been COVID-19, however, with all the lockdowns over the course of the past few years – including one lasting for over six months – which exposed to me the deepest vulnerabilities and the greatest strengths of my community. COVID-19 'woke' me to local citizens, me included, doing all we could to support local enterprise and vice versa, bound together by necessity. Working together because everyone benefits through collective action, and everyone can see it happening in real-time.

Strengthening community networks

COVID-19 also exposed the deep divide and inequalities within communities. For me, being able to access the open green spaces, national parks and beaches around me was vital for my mental wellbeing. But it also forced me to think about how other people in less fortunate locales were faring. The luxury I had of being able to support my local community is not the same experience for everyone.

And not just people and communities in far-off places, like Africa or the Pacific Islands. Communities elsewhere in the Sydney region, away from the coast, where population densities are greater, nature is scarcer, facilities are poorer, and heatwave temperatures go higher.

For those of us who can, we must lift each other up by investing our money to strengthen our local communities, our local businesses and produce, and local brands. And through supporting 'local', we can also address inequality and disadvantage, countering them with equity, compassion, and kindness, and supporting the local community through a shared sense of belonging and care.

Community food gardens are a beautiful example of how community connections are built. These shared spaces have such a range of benefits. They are good for our health, because we simultaneously have access to fresh fruits and veggies and to green open spaces. They allow families and individuals without outdoor space the opportunity to have a garden, and to feel soil between their fingers. They provide a sense of purpose and achievement, connect us to Country and allow us to learn, share and exchange knowledge across the cycle of the seasons.

Community also is strategic. Collective action makes sense when, for example, legal action is required, and taking it on as an individual is too costly or risky.

Just look at what happens when a community wins on climate. In a landmark ruling in 2021, Dutch citizens brought a case against Royal Dutch Shell for expanding its fossil fuels operations and neglecting its duty of care. The ruling ordered Shell to reduce its emissions by 45 per cent by 2030 from 2019 levels, described by *Forbes* as a 'monumental victory'.[60] Although Shell subsequently announced it is appealing the decision through the courts, nonetheless what a victory! Not just for the community from the Netherlands, but for the world.

In Australia, bushfire survivors who mobilised for climate action had their own landmark win after the NSW Land and Environment Court ruled that the state's Environment Protection Authority had a duty under law to take serious action on greenhouse gas emissions and climate change. My friend Jo Dodds, herself a bushfire survivor, took a leadership role on this for her community.

Every day, in my role as founder of 1 Million Women, I see women leading or participating in their communities, and doing it in a different way from men. Much more inclusive and consultative, typically with less ego.

It's not that all women lead like this, and I know some feel compelled to fight fire with fire, matching men at their own game to crack the glass ceiling. But I see women bringing their unique leadership skills to the table and making a real difference. Women who are not interested in the classic 'patriarchal and hierarchical' leadership model, because it doesn't work for them, and arguably doesn't really work for anyone in a community sense.

Before starting my 1 Million Women journey, I'd never really participated in anything like it. I'd never marched in the streets either. I'd never joined a local community group; never felt the need to fight for something I believed in. I was never that engaged with what was going on around me, and to be honest I didn't know I had a 'voice' on a societal challenge like climate change. I was a passionate person and a lover of life. I just didn't know I was powerful. Not until I had the courage to step outside of my comfort zone.

I had this overwhelming feeling of 'if not me then who?' I started 1 Million Women because I couldn't find what I was looking for. I had just changed my life, and I jumped on the internet to look for the next thing to do. I was so energised and excited by what I had just done with my life and in my household, but I couldn't find what I was looking for in terms of a community.

At the time, there seemed to be nothing speaking to me as a woman who wanted to be empowered on climate action. That intersection of women's empowerment and climate action just wasn't there. Well, not in Australia, anyway, so I decided to jump right in and build it myself.

I found my agency because of the support of the community of women around me. It wasn't leading from the top, it was much more a feeling of all being equals, and all harnessing our different skills towards a common good. I am 100 per cent sure 1 Million Women simply would not have happened without that spirit and support and strength of the community of women and men around me.

And although 1 Million Women is a community spread virtually across many cities and regions and countries, all the same principles apply when you are engaging locally with others.

I asked our 1 Million Women community the question: 'What does community mean to you?' The theme running through everyone's replies was the same. It's about inclusiveness; about a shared common goal. It's about outcomes. Here is a taste of what was said:

- Community that lives in close proximity to me, but it also means like-minded individuals working towards a common goal.
- Community is the village which supports all in times of need, and more importantly offers a chance for those with excess (time, provisions, skills, knowledge and so much more) to share with their fellow community members.
- To me, a community is a human ecosystem. It's a place where you have a part to play (even if you don't know what it is yet) and it thrives through cooperation and compassion.

- For me, community is the bank of goodwill that ensures we all move forward together and nobody gets left behind. People coming together to help make where they live a better place.
- Looking out for one another. Realising your actions have consequences on others around you. Being aware of what is happening in your neighbourhood.
- Community = Active Inclusivity = Zero Exclusivity.

Call to action: Everything we do to act on climate at a local level – in our street, our neighbourhood, our town – has a ripple effect going out into the world.

- Find out what's happening around you.
- Join a local group standing up to the politician who doesn't genuinely represent you.
- Support local business as best you can.
- Join in on community activities and let that connection propel you to the next.

If there's something you're passionate about making happen in your locale, remember, you could be the first! You could start a local community group yourself. You don't need to have all the answers, you just need to be passionate about something you care about enough to start acting.

The way ahead isn't always prepared for us, ready to travel on, but that shouldn't stop us from doing it ourselves and paving the way for others. So much of the time we can feel like we have no idea what we're doing, and yet we end up realising we're far more capable than we thought. We need to believe in ourselves, while drawing strength from others and sharing the highs and the lows. That's the spirit of community.

10
NEW DAWN FOR POLITICS

It's no surprise women are leading the charge with politically engaged communities as well. I keep meeting women who tell me they've had enough of the self-serving crap and lies from politicians. I'm one of those women too. We are angry and fed up.

Our politicians are meant to genuinely serve the people, to serve us. They are meant to represent their communities, to be voices for the people in their electorates and not just to regurgitate the party line. We all see how that's working out, and women aren't standing for it.

We cannot be passive players in our communities if our politicians aren't representing our values. In particular, politicians who fail to put climate action at the top of the agenda should not be controlling our future. We have a real say in this: the democratic way to send this message is through the ballot box. In this decade, we need courageous and bold politicians. The power to elect them, and hold them to account, lies with us: the people who vote.

Politicians who fail to put climate action at the top of the agenda should not be controlling our future.

Democracy is meaningless if we don't do the numbers ourselves, standing up when our political representatives forget they serve us and bind their allegiances to political parties or, even worse, to vested interests. We need to show them we are intolerant not just of outright corruption, but also the blurring of lines between civic duty and private or ideological interests.

When it comes to politics, climate action and decision-making based on evidence go together as values we can hold politicians to if they want our votes.

Politicians will change course if enough people in their constituency pressure them to, putting their jobs on the line. Letter writing, petitions, electorate office visits and having many conversations with your elected local member, either individually or with others in your local community, are all part of the democratic to-do list. But we need to accelerate our efforts to put 1.5°C, and resetting our world by 2030, firmly at the top of the agenda.

Luckily, grassroots community organisers are already mustering their resources, with women leading the way. It's exhilarating to watch this unfold – a demonstration of community spirit that is as inspirational as it is powerful.

Striking out for independents

Here is how it all started, at least in its contemporary manifestation. While there's a history of male independents in Australia's national parliament, a new women's story in this space really only kicked off less than a decade ago and it's attracting women in unprecedented numbers.

In 2013, Cathy McGowan AO got herself elected to the seat of Indi (a federal electorate in the state of Victoria's northeast) through the strength of her team's community-level organising, which began with the formation of the 'Voices of Indi' grassroots campaign to engage the local community through kitchen-table conversations. Cathy was both the first independent MP for Indi, and the first female independent MP to sit on the crossbench of the Australian Parliament.

Cathy's successful grassroots campaigns sparked nationwide interest in the potential of community-based, independent politicians to chart a new course for Australian democracy.

What is so powerful about the grassroots organising structure Cathy used is that it's malleable. Now there are dozens of 'Voices of ...' groups around Australia. There is a tried and proven formula to follow, yet each one of these 'Voices of ...' community groups is created in subtly different ways, bringing the skills of the people and the local issues of each community to the table.

Zali Steggall, the independent MP for the New South Wales federal electorate of Warringah, near where I live, ran against former Prime Minister Tony Abbott, and won her seat on the strength of spectacular community organising based on the 'Voices of ...' template.

The community network was created first, building an early groundswell of support across the electorate. People who wouldn't normally get involved in politics got involved. People who'd never volunteered before showed up. The joy of being part of something big, and the momentum, which kept building, captured the community. And this was all before the candidate was announced or even found. People wanted change.

My friend Dr Samantha Graham, the founder of State of Mind, which runs capability development programs for individuals and leadership teams, is another long-time climate campaigner.

Sam tells me: 'Women are leading the charge because they are allowing themselves to feel, and to express, their anger, their fury, their rage – and channelling that into something positive to effect change.'

Women are waking up to the impacts of climate change particularly because we care for the young, the poor and the elderly. We see the impacts more readily in our children's and grandchildren's often-unspoken anxiety, despair and curtailed futures. Cathy McGowan explained it to me this way:

Taking inspiration, and then using your knowledge and your skills to do something in your own community, is what's making this movement work. Because there's no recipe. There are principles and values, but as soon as you say it to people and particularly to women, they go, 'Oh, I know how to do that', and away they're off and running.

We met all these new people who we really liked, who we didn't know. And there was energy that came out of all those new connections. I know it exists and it's always happened, but putting the energy into politics was such a productive place for our energy to go, because so often we've been arguing, you know, outside the tent. So on climate, there's groups all over the place now actually doing, not waiting for the government anymore to do stuff.

In my own federal electorate of Mackellar, on Garigal land in Sydney's Northern Beaches, Sophie Scamps and Anyo Geddes have been inspired by Cathy McGowan's leadership. They were part of the founding team of Voices for Mackellar, then co-founded Mackellar Rising to mount a political insurgency. They stepped into the unknown, and into their own agency, after feeling deeply frustrated over the lack of leadership from the government on climate.

As a local, I've watched these two amazing women step into this space with power and determination. Sophie, a GP who subsequently has declared as an Independent candidate running for Mackellar in the 2022 Australian elections on a platform of climate, integrity and health, told me:

I was trying to convince other people that they needed to lead on this, and then I had a sort of revelation. Why not me? And it was really amazing when the rhetoric changed from 'I really want to do this thing' and people saying, 'Yeah, that's a great idea', to, 'We're doing this thing', to people saying, 'How can I help?' And that's where it all kicked off. You meet people in your community that you never knew and there is energy that comes from that.

This is where courage comes in. Cathy McGowan calls it our 'courage muscle'. It's far easier to do nothing, or wait for someone else, so we need our courage now. I hear that a lot, where people have gone, 'Someone else will step up and do it.' And then no one's doing it. So you go, 'Okay, I have to do it.'

Jumping feet-first into politics

Earlier in this book we canvassed how, as women, we are often confronted by the unknown, and the spaces we may not usually step into, or have been excluded from. It is so much easier to jump into the unknown when you are part of a community and when you've got other people around you.

You find it easier to step out of your comfort zone and just do things that you may not have done before, because you've got everybody lifting you up. And although the original 'Voices of ...' movement didn't start out to be a gendered thing, it has fallen that way. Cathy McGowan says:

Being a candidate and running a political campaign is not for everybody. And one of the things that I've discovered about this way of working is that it gives women, I think, an equal playing field to the blokes. You know, it's not designed to do that. But because it's community-based and it's very different from how the parties do stuff, it enables ambitious, clever, intelligent, well-connected women to find a leadership niche.

In 2022, in the lead-up to a national election campaign, the Voices movement has grown across Australia. Women, and men too, are stepping up. But it's predominantly women, and climate action is the No. 1 issue they are running on. At last count there were 33 official 'Voices of ...' communities creating a new style of politicians who have their constituency at their heart, are fighting for a better world, and are putting climate action at the centre of their campaigns and their agendas.

Anyo Geddes, from Mackellar Rising, tells me:

The Voices movement goes beyond elections, beyond candidates. Genuine community voices are something that the newspapers and the major parties can't attack. 'Who are all these people who actually care about their kids and their future and their community? What's wrong with them?' It doesn't make sense. So one of the most powerful things about this is that it's people, real people, real communities getting together, participating in a better democracy for themselves and their children.

And that's something that can be ongoing beyond election cycles.

In our most recent 1 Million Women election survey, early in 2022, 94 per cent of female respondents supported climate action measures to ramp up Australia's emissions reduction targets for 2030. They will be voting to increase renewable energy and phase out burning coal, oil and gas. A big majority, 88 per cent, said they will be voting for a candidate who will represent their views and their values when they vote in the Australian Parliament.

The Voices movement, and the trend towards female independents more broadly, are templates for communities across the world to explore, adapt and adopt. As voters for urgent climate action in this decade and holding the 1.5°C line, values-driven independents give us more choice at election time. They are not locked into the agenda of a major political party, whatever the ideology that drives them.

Creating change from within

Independents aren't the only way to drive change through democratic systems. We need to change the political mainstream as well, particularly within the major parties that typically form governments. We need to spread our influence to all parts of the political spectrum to elevate climate action to the top of the agenda. The goal is bipartisan support for decisive climate action; this has been broadly achieved in some nations, including the UK and a number of European countries, but not in others such as Australia and the US. Destructive climate wars between major parties have blocked progress, and conflict means delay, which the world can't afford. This must stop in order to carve out ambitious targets with accelerated climate action to achieve them.

We all can play an important role by being proactive. We need to find and support the political champions who are willing to bring this about within their own parties. Those politicians who will do all they can to influence their political peers. Politicians who won't ignore the science and the evidence all around us. Who are courageous enough to fight for climate action, even if it goes against the prevailing party line. Politicians who embrace our optimism for a better world and heed our determination to fight for 1.5°C. Who will do all they can to shift the status quo within their own parties, and who will stand for this in their electorates.

As communities, and as voters, we can contribute to changing the hearts and minds of our politicians. Our voices are powerful. Our vote counts. So does the pressure we put on our politicians, and through the conversations we have with them, and our honesty in telling them what we expect in exchange for our vote.

For myself, I am totally clear on this: no politician today should be in power anywhere on this planet if they are failing to elevate climate action to the top of their agenda. I will champion those courageous politicians who will speak up and do all they can to shift the mindsets of their political collegues. Those politicians who want to bring about bipartisan support at a pace we have never seen before regardless of who is in government. This gives me clarity and strength when I get the opportunity to engage politicians.

None of us should feel disenfranchised. We have choices. If you are a committed supporter of one of the major parties, even a paid-up party member, you can do all you can to campaign inside the party and have those conversations for the climate action we need. Whether you are inside a party tent or outside, the point is making climate action your No. 1 issue.

Call to action: Every election in this decade anywhere in the world, whether it be local, state or national, shapes where we will be by 2030. Every year counts. Every politician counts. Every vote counts. Every conversation on climate with our local political representatives counts. Women's participation counts. Make climate action non-negotiable for your vote.

No politician today should be in power anywhere on this planet if they are failing to elevate climate action to the top of their agenda.

When election time comes around, make sure you know where all the parties and candidates stand on climate. Have as many conversations as you can with other women in your local community. Influence as many people as you can to vote 1 for climate action.

And in between elections, engage your locally elected political representatives, and the prospective candidates, on the importance of this critical decade and on climate action for your local area. Be present. Get engaged. Never be silent.

11

THE DAY-TO-DAY STUFF

Climate change is deeply personal, and needs to affect the choices we make every single day. Each of us should strive to leave the lowest possible personal footprint on the planet. The cumulative power of millions and billions of us taking lifestyle actions every day should not be underestimated!

The really good news is that people are acting, and challenging the culture of overconsumption and waste – putting solar on their rooftops, being energy efficient, rejecting single-use plastics and overpackaging, and minimising food waste. This story has shifted so much in the last 10 years, and to me that's tremendously exciting.

I put up a question on 1 Million Women's Instagram and Facebook channels, asking our community: 'What is one climate action in your life that makes you feel powerful?'

We received over 600 comments in just a few hours. The 1MW Community responded with all manner of things they were doing in their lives. While there were far too many to list them all here, let me share some:

- Lining my kitchen bin with newspaper and then tying it up with twine to pop in the bin.
- Having a native beehive in my backyard.
- Not buying fast fashion.
- Mindful shopping, avoiding plastic and excess packaging.
- Eating less meat.
- Changing to an ethical super.
- Composting.
- Not owning a tumble dryer.
- Growing my own food and sharing it with family, friends and neighbours.
- Riding a bike instead of owning a car.
- Planting trees.
- Getting the gas cut off.
- Not buying something in the first place.
- Installing solar panels.

- Repairing everything.
- Teaching my daughter all I've learned to save our Earth and the importance of it.
- Buying 95 per cent of my fruit and veggies and other food from local farmers' markets every week.
- Picking up rubbish everywhere I go.
- Talking to young people on the things we can do.
- Being a conscious consumer.
- Sewing waste fabric scraps from designer houses into useful items.
- Refusing single use plastics.
- Not owning a car.
- Working with kids at my neighbourhood school.
- Buying local goods.
- Living within my means.
- Using reusable sanitary towels.
- Switching to a green bank.
- Being a vegetarian.
- Being a vegan.
- Applying the 'no waste' concept to all aspects of my life.
- Turning my green waste into worm-food.
- Using public transport.
- Gardening without chemicals.

- Using renewable energy.
- Taking quick, cool showers.
- Upcycling upholstery.
- Voting.
- Educating others on ethical banks.
- Never going to a gas station again.
- Love my EV xx.
- Swapping all my plastic to glass or fabric.
- Regularly monitoring my carbon footprint.
- Buying second hand.
- Coastal clean-ups.
- Voting with my money as much as possible.
- Buying only preloved.
- Eating more plant-based foods.
- Mending and refashioning my own clothes.

I love the variety in all of this, and the simplicity of the things which make you feel powerful. Acting in our own lives, no matter how small that action is, gives us agency. It's like a secret superpower of behaviour change.

Action helps us take ownership of any issue. It helps our mental health when we take positive steps to mitigating some of the causes of climate anxiety, and a quick win can keep you optimistic.

Small changes add up to something big

When it comes to profoundly changing the way we live, all of the small and large actions add up. Everything we do to stop greenhouse gas pollution from entering the atmosphere is reducing the heating pressure on the planet.

Right now, we live in a culture of consumerism that has gone into overdrive. Plastic has become a major environmental threat – its early promise has morphed into a nightmare of single-use convenience.

According to the United Nations, a million plastic drinking bottles are purchased around the world every five minutes, while five *trillion* single-use plastic bags are used worldwide every year.

A million plastic drinking bottles are purchased around the world every five minutes.

In total, half of all the plastic produced is designed to only be used once and then be thrown away, and 99 per cent of it is made from fossil fuels. Coca-Cola alone produces one billion throwaway plastic bottles each year. That's 3400 every second.[61] And of all the plastic being produced globally, only 9 per cent gets recycled into something else.

While bioplastics pose their own logistical issues, plastics made from corn, sugar cane or potatoes can reduce a dependence on fossil fuels. The Dutch Government, in 2019, launched its Plastic Pact, with the Ministry of Infrastructure and the Environment partnering with grocery chains, brand owners, packaging manufacturers, plastic recyclers and environmental organisations to reduce the use of plastics by the year 2050.[62]

Cooperation between government departments, plastic producers and environmental groups is key in tackling the issue of plastics at a structural level. We can learn a lot from the Dutch and lobby our own politicians to make a Plastic Pact possible.

What's inside your Tupperware?

While plastic containers are used to seal food to keep it fresh, food is a huge issue in its own right. There's a range of estimates about exactly how much food waste contributes to climate change, but food production and waste falls between a quarter and a third of total greenhouse gas pollution globally.

The study Our World In Data puts this figure at more than one-quarter (26 per cent) of total emissions, coming from a variety of sources:[63] deforestation and land use change (think land clearing to make way for farming and grazing), emissions from fertilisers and manure, methane from cattle on the livestock side and rice production on the plant-based agriculture side, energy use on the farm, supply chain emissions from food processing, storage refrigeration, and transport.[64]

A recent scientific report in *The Guardian* put the contribution of total global food production at one-third of all greenhouse gas emissions associated with human activity, and beef alone made up one-quarter of the food share. Beef is by far the most carbon-intensive food on a per kilogram of food product basis, at 99.48 kg of CO_2-e (carbon dioxide equivalent), compared with 9.87 kg for poultry and just 3.16 kg for tofu, which is made from soybeans.[65] So beef produces 10 times as much carbon emissions as chicken and 30 times as much as tofu, illustrating the power of our food choices for climate action.

The 2021 Meat Atlas report details how global industrial meat production is increasing, and its message to wealthier countries is clear: we must halve our meat consumption in this decade to keep pace with action on climate.[66]

Whether or not you embrace being a vegetarian or vegan, or whether you simply reduce your meat consumption, food choices make a big difference. And spending the same amount of money on half the amount of meat means that you can support ethical and local suppliers with transparent production chains.

Decarbonisation is key

In this defining decade, we know that every sector of society must decarbonise. The food sector, the fashion industry, mining, manufacturing, transport, energy, real estate, telcos and big data, finance and insurance; our interconnected society means that even the least likely industries emit carbon dioxide somehow.

And industry leaders are beginning to understand that fossil fuels are on the way out. There is an explosion of innovation, ingenuity and creativity happening across all sectors at the moment, which we can collectively throw our weight behind.

Electric vehicles are part of the electrify-everything equation, and a great example in their own right of how change is taking off. Ideally running on clean electricity from renewables, EVs are starting to push out fossil fuel-powered internal combustion engine vehicles when it comes to mechanical design.

In Norway – the world's leading country for EV uptake – electric vehicle purchasing may reach between 80 and 100 per cent during 2022, potentially three years ahead of the Norwegian Government's 2025 target.[67] The whole world needs to speed up on the transition to EVs, starting with wealthy nations like Australia. Governments can change policies, set targets and create incentives, especially when there is pressure on them to do so.

There's almost no area of our daily lives where we can't find ways to reduce our footprint. We have already talked about overconsumption, but here are three more big areas where we can have an enormous impact; where we have big opportunities to downsize our footprint: the food we waste, the money we invest and the energy we use.

Leftovers have to go somewhere

Many of us simply don't see the direct link between climate change and the food we waste. Whether it's the thousands of kilometres our food must travel before it gets to us, the produce that supermarkets reject for mainly cosmetic reasons, the food we allow to go off before we get around to eating it, the food we cook that we don't eat or any number of other ways food is wasted, it all adds up to more greenhouse gas pollution.

So much wasted food finds its way into our bins then goes to landfill, where it rots and produces methane – the potent greenhouse gas which the IPCC's 'Code Red' report warns is on its way to rivalling carbon dioxide in terms of global heating potential.

Before I got the point about climate change, I simply didn't think too hard about how much food was going into the bin. I always served too much at dinnertime, and never had a plan for our leftovers. It didn't occur to me to go shopping in my own fridge before heading to the supermarket, and when I did buy food, I rarely kept to a pre-planned list. And on lazy nights I bought takeaway, even though I needed to use up what I already had.

I was shocked to find out that an estimated 40 per cent of fruit and vegetable produce gets rejected by supermarkets because it doesn't pass the 'beauty test' – no spots and blemishes, no strange shapes, and all looking the same. These days, I'm a regular shopper for 'imperfect' produce and I really appreciate the stores which offer it as a discounted option, giving me the choice.

But food waste is avoidable: 70 per cent of it could be avoided without a great deal of effort and behaviour change on our part. Better still, when we aren't wasting food, it saves us money, and it's looking after the planet, and it's being respectful to the food's origins and our farmers, graziers, fishers, horticulturalists and other food producers.

A greater sense of respect for our food, and the land and the water where it grows, and the people who produce it, is fundamental for resetting our world. There is such a big disconnect between urban populations and rural ones, and this makes those of us who live in the cities and the suburbs lose respect for and even awareness of the food's story, including where it comes from and who grows it. We've

A greater sense of respect for our food, and the land and the water where it grows, and the people who produce it, is fundamental for resetting our world.

become disconnected from our food's authenticity, seasonality and provenance, and this means we devalue the food itself and don't care enough to avoid wasting it.

When we meet the farmers and the producers at a farmers' market, we hear their stories, we connect with their challenges and it makes us appreciate their produce so much more. When we grow our own food in backyard gardens, or on our apartment balconies, or in a community garden, we can appreciate the care, skill and effort required to produce food in the quantity and quality we need. Food is profoundly important, yet in our throwaway society, we've managed to trivialise it to the extent we can waste it with barely a second thought.

Through 1 Million Women, I've done a lot of work with the innovative 'Love Food Hate Waste' campaign, which was pioneered in the United Kingdom, then brought to Australia by the New South Wales Government.

It's helped me to understand how easy it is in our busy lives to just scrape food into the bin without thinking or realising that you are scraping away all those foods' origin stories, as well as the resources, the time, the energy, the transport and all the hard work and effort that went into getting the food from farm to plate.

Not to mention that when we waste food in the privileged world, it disrespects and undermines efforts to help billions of people who go hungry regularly, or are unable to afford a healthy diet for their households, or who may be actively starving.

Honouring our food, and respecting how it's grown and where it travelled from to make its way to our plates, helps us resist the temptation of waste. It helps us understand the brutal challenges our farmers are facing because of climate change. It acknowledges that food security is a global issue, and how a disrupted climate system affects the food system on every level, through drought, flooding, heatwaves, extreme weather events and bushfires.

I've made a point of going out to farms and meeting farmers wherever I can, which sometimes has meant online in the COVID-19 era. Scientist and author Anika Molesworth, who farms in far-western New South Wales, is poetic in describing her experience as a farmer facing up to the climate crisis, and describes how the food waste story can start while still on the farm:

Where I live is a starkly beautiful part of the country. Ruby red soils and sapphire blue skies. It's expansive, low intensity grazing land here, and because it is so dry and so hot, it's actually quite challenging farmland. We grow sheep and goats on our property but because we've been in drought for nearly five years now we've had to sell all of our livestock, and we're just working on protecting the vegetation and the water resources and carrying the landscape through these really challenging times.

Climate change impacts farmers in a huge amount of ways and contributes to that story of food loss and wastage. For example, climate change increases the frequency and intensity of extreme weather events like storms, floods and droughts.

Hail at the wrong time of year can flatten the crop. And so all of that produce is wasted. The same goes if there is a flood and a road gets cut off, and the trucks can't get there to pick up the pumpkins or the apples. That food gets wasted. Combating climate change is probably one of the most important things we can do to ensure that we can carry that food from the paddock right through to the plate and not see that wastage at the farm end of the system.

This food waste costs the global economy nearly $US940 billion every year,[68] almost a trillion dollars. Just imagine if that amount of money were going into climate solutions instead of wasted produce! If food waste were a country, it would be the third largest emitter of greenhouse gases in the world. New data shows that 10 per cent of global greenhouse gas emissions comes from wasted food[69] – that's three times the emissions from aviation everywhere.

This is such a big issue, and a great place to start mobilising. The UN's Sustainable Development Goals includes halving per capita global food waste at retail and consumer levels by 2030. We can all play our part and get involved through the food system as consumers of food, as households, as farmers, as producers and as concerned citizens of the planet paying attention to every part of the food story.

Our first goal can be to reduce our food waste by half at a household and personal level, starting right now, and making sure any food we don't eat is still useful and not going to landfill.

Our first goal can be to reduce our food waste by half at a household and personal level, starting right now, and making sure any food we don't eat is still useful and not going to landfill.

Composting is a great recycling system – and it does wonders for the garden. If you have the space, you can get a worm farm or some chickens. If space is tight, a good option for you might be a small bokashi system to transform your food scraps into nourishing compost.

In any case, we can all determine our portion sizes to reflect how hungry we actually feel, responding to our body's needs and not a preset idea of what our meals should look like.

Use up what's in the fridge before buying more. Have an *eat me first basket* in the fridge to remind you. We can shop to a list, grow our own and buy what's in season, checking best-by and use-by dates, and planning our meals accordingly. We can freeze food we don't eat straight away, and learn other ways to store food to make it last longer. We can do everything possible to prevent food ending up in our bins and appreciate and honour the food being produced for us.

Money matters

It wasn't until three years into running 1 Million Women that I realised my bank and superfund were investing my money in the fossil fuel industry. It's so obvious now, but I'd never thought it through. How counterproductive, and how disconnected this was from my values. There I was, thinking I was the climate warrior. I'd already done the hard work of transforming my life, or so I thought.

Because it's mandatory in Australia to have a super fund, we often pick one and then forget about it, not actively thinking of it as an investment. But silently, there in the background, I was still supporting coal, oil and gas with my money, letting others make choices that went against my values. I did my research and switched my day-to-day banking and my super fund, and then eventually our home mortgage account too.

Now my money supports low-carbon investments and renewable energy, and it is the best feeling ever. It means better investments too, because I am not exposed to industries which have to be shut down fast to respond to the urgency of the climate crisis.

Back before I got the point on climate change, as an adult earning a living, I never once questioned my bank or my super fund to see if they aligned with my values. I never thought to ask if they invested in the tobacco industry or in gambling, deforestation or even weapons!

A survey we did with 1200 of our 1 Million Women members a few years ago clearly showed that understanding the climate impacts of our financial arrangements, and having the appetite to do anything about it, was at the bottom of pretty much everyone's pile. So we've spent the last three years telling this story over and over again, and educating our community about the power of our money and the choices we can make.

Now, when I'm out and about speaking on panels and at events, I am happy to report that the first questions I get are often about divestment from fossil fuels. When I unexpectedly made it to Glasgow COP26 in November 2021, during a brief window between pandemic waves, I was included on a side-conference panel called 'Money Matters'. It's a critical issue for our critical decade, and each of our investment dollars, accumulated into powerful funds, can help to change the world.

Money matters, and women's money matters. Globally, women's wealth has shown unprecedented growth over the last decade. Women now control 32 per cent of the world's wealth, according to the Boston Consulting Group.[70] This will rise at a compound annual growth rate of 5.7 per cent to $US97 trillion by 2024.

It's big numbers like this which lead me to believe that our world already has all the money it needs to reinvent itself and create a new system in which sustainability pays its own way, rewarding us all.

When it comes to our super and our banking, we can make sure that where we invest our money aligns with our values, and supports all of humanity and future generations. This is a transition story we can all be part of, here and now, and forever.

We can shift our money to financial institutions only investing in renewable and low-carbon projects and the good things for our planet. Or we can shift to a green fund in the fund we are already in, if we can see that they are making plans for change across their portfolio, and then influence the financial institution to do more or go faster.

And we can influence others to do the same, by sharing our own stories. We need to mobilise the bulk of the economy to change the way we are all investing.

Emma Herd is the Oceania Partner for Climate Change with EY, one of the world's biggest accounting firms, and is a former CEO of the Investor Group on Climate Change, which represents investors with over $AUD2 trillion in funds in Australia and New Zealand, and $AUD20 trillion globally.

Emma, who has been working in the financial sector for over 20 years, lives and breathes investment for climate action:

How do we use our influence and power to get financial institutions to change and rebalance their portfolio, by decreasing the amount that they have invested in fossil fuels and increasing the amount that they have in low-carbon solutions?

Switching financial institutions is powerful. It supports those institutions that won't invest in fossil fuels. But power can also come from influencing the financial companies you are with. If you switch within the fund you are with, then that incentivizes the fund to create more low-carbon options and to have more of the portfolio invested in climate solutions.

Money is important, which means any greenwashing by financial institutions is important too. When it comes to financial greenwashing, we need to be constantly vigilant, just as we need to pay close attention to the financial performance of the investment companies we entrust our money to.

We need to make sure that any financial institution we deal with has genuine 2030 transition plans, meaning that they are acting in this critical decade, and are expanding their green and climate-friendly offerings as well as their own performance.

Genuinely eco-friendly businesses will provide easily accessible information on their production and company values. There are also growing numbers of watchdog organisations tracking climate and sustainability performance by financial institutions, and other sectors as well, and it's easy to search a company's reputation online before committing to them.

According to the 'Banking on Climate Chaos' report in 2022, produced by a coalition of campaign groups, in the six years since the Paris Agreement set the world on the quest to hold the 1.5°C line, the world's 60 biggest banks have poured $US4.6 triilion into fossil fuel investments.[71]

It sounds like a lot of money, and it is, but it's also money that ultimately belongs to people like us. In Australia, superannuation assets totalled $AUD3.4 trillion at the end of the September 2021 quarter.[72] According to investment analysts, if all of this super were invested in low-carbon and ethical products, we would save 78 million tonnes of carbon dioxide-equivalent emissions, which is like taking 16.9 million petrol cars off the road, or saving the average emissions from 4.6 million Australian households.[73]

By 2025, it's estimated that the women of Australia will hold $AUD1.5 trillion in superannuation, yet population-wise Australia is only a small country of 25 million people. In America, it's projected women will control $US30 trillion in funds by 2030.[74] So, globally, funds held by women are already a vast resource for change, and growing rapidly. And these days, as well as investing for climate action, you can even choose investments with a 'gender lens', targeting companies with more women in their leadership teams and on their board.[75]

Just imagine what we could do with this much money, well invested to target climate action this decade. The financial marketplace is beginning to catch on, with many more products and providers that don't invest in fossil fuels than we've seen until recent years, and good advisers too. (I am not a financial adviser, and consistent with standard practice you will need to do all your own research on this, and seek professional advice as you require, before making or changing any investments.)

Energy efficiency begins at home

The moment I realised I was powerful was when I got our household electricity consumption down by 20 per cent and saw that I had saved money and pollution simultaneously. It was the low hanging fruit. It wasn't hard. I was being more vigilant around the house, and learning exactly what in our household was guzzling the most energy. We didn't have air conditioning, which is often the biggest one, but we did (I stress 'did') have a tumble dryer – and a dryer alone can account for 12 per cent of typical household energy use.

Now our home, the same home where I started my energy saving, is effectively net zero emissions for electricity, including net zero emissions for running a 100 per cent electric car on electricity from the solar panels on our rooftop. Any electrons from our solar which we don't use ourselves flow out to the local electricity system and supply clean energy to neighbours nearby, more than offsetting any fossil fuel-generated power we take from the grid at night. How wonderful is that?

Back in 2007, early in my journey, there were roughly only 7000 rooftop solar systems in Australia. Now there are over 3 million homes and businesses generating their own clean electricity from the sun, and momentum is still building. This is the power of people who haven't waited for politicians to tell them what to do, and who instead have gone out and invested their own money in a form of climate action, even if for some their main motivation is saving money rather than environmental protection.

Renewables are set to account for 95 per cent of the net increase in new global power generation capacity through to the end of 2026, according to the International Energy

Agency.[76] A transformative global reset for energy is within reach by 2030 or soon after.

Within my country, as pressure for long overdue political action builds, we'll inevitably be electrifying nearly everything, while shutting down coal-fired power stations and phasing out the massive cost burden of importing oil-based fuels like petrol and diesel for transport.

The energy transformation underway is unstoppable and we can all be part of it, one way or another. We can buy low-carbon appliances and ditch the energy-sucking tumble dryer for clothesline and sunshine instead. For those with swimming pools, we can run the pool pump an hour less every day.

The energy transformation underway is unstoppable and we can all be part of it.

It's easy and free to turn the lights off when they are not needed, sealing all the gaps in the house will keep the cold drafts out in winter and stop cooled air escaping in summer, and turning all standby power off could save 10 per cent of wasted household energy. And so on and so on!

We can put solar panels on our rooftops if possible, or join a local community energy project, like a solar garden, if not; find a bulk-buying initiative, or a microgrid; or opt for green power from our energy providers. We can switch to a community-based energy provider that invests in renewable energy projects; or simply get better at being energy efficient and eliminating waste.

In the last 10 years, Australians have seen community energy projects popping up all over the country. People are gathering their collective power to create sustainable communities, zero emission communities, and 100 per cent renewable communities. All of this community-level mobilisation helps to cut carbon, and goes to where we need to be by 2030. There are so many of these groups, each taking real action and creating great stories to tell.

Gemma Meier is a farmer from Grong Grong in the Murray-Darling Basin, Australia's agricultural heartland. Alongside crops and livestock, her farm will soon host a community solar investment project called Haystacks.

Sitting by the campfire under the stars one night on her property, Gemma explained to me that for a long time she felt deeply distressed about climate change, and felt powerless to do anything about it. But that feeling changed when she began to work with the KOMO Energy and the not-for-profit Community Power Agency and created Haystacks.[77]

It's a virtual community solar energy project giving access to solar power to people who can't put solar panels on their own rooftops. Gemma sectioned off four hectares of her land where a solar garden will be built, and available plots will be sold to to 'solar gardeners' who may live hundreds or even thousands of kilometres away. Each plot mimics a mid-sized 3kW home solar system on your roof, fully exporting to the grid. So wherever they live, the solar gardeners harvest the clean energy benefit from their nearest power supply.

Given that one-third of Australians rent their homes, with a similar figure for other countries around the world like Spain, Ireland, USA and the UK where homeownership is steadily dropping, there are more and more people who don't have the freedom to get solar panels installed who still want to be able to use renewable energy. And there are apartment owners or households or small businesses that can't access solar for whatever reason.

Projects like Haystacks offer a real opportunity for everyone to have access to solar, and demonstrate that community-owned and small-scale solar farms are viable, replicable, and provide multiple economic and community benefits for everyone involved.

While it's important to keep our electricity use down in the face of increasing extremes of temperature – more heatwaves and record hot days – doing all we can to make homes more energy efficient in the first place will help us through. Many Australian houses are built for European climates, but clever retrofitting can greatly increase their comfort and liveability without creating even greater reliance on artificial heating and cooling.

We can find ways to use natural ventilation and high energy-efficiency cooling, taking advantage of natural air flow. By choosing a lighter coloured, more reflective roof when we build, we can reduce the temperature in a house by 10 per cent during a heatwave, and reduce the urban heat effect in the local area at the same time. Lots of trees in our gardens and streetscapes help with local cooling as well.

A recent article from Australia's public broadcaster, the ABC, carried the headline, 'The way we use air conditioning is changing, and it's time we talked about it.'[78] We need the media to constantly highlight changes we can make to adapt to the climate change we can't stop, including the way we cool our homes in a hotter climate.

Once again, there's a COVID-19 and climate connection. People are at home more, they want the air in their homes to be healthy, and they need to stay cool when the temperature climbs, and climbs. This particular article explained that COVID-19 and climate change were making people worry about the air in their homes being healthy – a concern for those who have lived through bushfire events as well.

In early 2022, *The Sydney Morning Herald* reported on a Penrith woman, in Sydney's summer heat-prone west, taking refuge with her child in a car to use its air conditioning. The article introduced a non-profit urban campaign group called Sweltering Cities, which has a mission to pressure politicians to take rising heat levels seriously as a public health threat.[79] Extreme heat exacerbates pre-existing conditions such as heart and kidney disease, as well as affecting vulnerable people such as children and the elderly who are especially prone to heat illness.[80]

My dear friend Rachel Kyte, the climate policy expert who's now a university dean, recently gave a Ted Talk titled 'How to provide cooling for everyone – without warming the planet'. She succinctly lays out the issue that cooling our homes and buildings is heating up the planet too, and she highlights the global inequality when it comes to staying cool. I urge you to listen to it, but here is a taste:

Most wealthy people can stay cool. They often live in wealthy leafy suburbs with an air conditioner and a generator out back, and they have cool offices, cool schools and hospitals. But many people on low incomes live and work in urban concrete jungles void of green space and shade, or live in rural areas ...

Almost a billion people live without energy access today. Billions more live without access to reliable energy, and 2.3 billion can only afford a highly inefficient or polluting air conditioner ... The solutions go well beyond just fixing air conditioning. The solutions range from city design to architecture, from building materials to appliances, from geoengineering to green roofs. The solutions can be high tech, they can be low tech.[81]

Our cities, globally, are crucial to climate action. Cities only take up 2 per cent of the earth's surface, but 78 per cent of the world's energy is consumed by this 2 per cent.[82] Once again, women are on the frontline. Up to 30 per cent of the population in some European countries cannot afford sufficient fuel for indoor heating. Women, especially single mothers and elderly women, constitute the majority of this 30 per cent. There is a lack of female representation in the energy sector, so it follows that there is a lack of gender expertise in decision-making.

Every action we take, from day-to-day activities to the big lifestyle choices, matters.

Call to action: Just act. Every single molecule of greenhouse gas pollution that we can prevent from entering the atmosphere in this decade matters. Every action we take, from day-to-day activities to the big lifestyle choices, matters. Every solar panel, every community energy project, every kilo of food waste we prevent from going to landfill matters. Every dollar we invest in renewable projects through our super funds and banks matters more than anything. The rejection of single-use plastic, the reduction of red meat consumption, the energy-efficient home, the car pool, the walking bus or the 100 per cent electric vehicle journey matters.

Every person you can influence to cut carbon matters too. The millions of actions we are taking collectively, every single day, between this very moment and 2030 matter like our lives depend on it.

12
A NEW WORLD

I've always felt that 1 Million Women has played a very specific role in making sure we don't feel alone, especially in the times when despair threatens to overwhelm our courage.

We make sure our communications are filled with optimism and joy and strength, and the power of the collective. Simply taking action and keeping going sits at the heart of our theory of change. We don't wait for governments, or big business and brands, or anyone else. We just get on with it.

Our 1 Million Women community is like the heartbeat that gives back, pulse for pulse. It's the circular flow thing again. Every blog, every interaction, every piece of engagement, every campaign helps me understand how our community is feeling at any given moment. Whether it is hope, optimism, excitement or feeling energised with a climate win; or being overwhelmed, sad, despairing at the latest climate news; we listen and hear, we respond, and we steer back towards optimism and action.

Beyond acting right now, and resetting our world by 2030, lies a bigger picture. My optimism and my mission are underpinned by a vision for a new world, one we have the opportunity to create if we respond to the climate crisis at the speed and the scale, and with the determination it compels in this decade.

This is a world in which people and the planet co-exist sustainably with integrity, fairness, inclusiveness, gender equality and justice, with diversity woven into the fabric of our existence. And with climate action and care for Mother Earth at the front and centre, always.

Our decade of action is so critical because, if the world is going to hold the 1.5°C line for average temperature rise, we have to be doing it *now*.

We've gone past 1.2°C already, and as Professor Lesley Hughes' analysis of the IPCC scientific report in 2021 spells out, on our current trajectory we could exceed 1.5°C as early as 2032. So we can't wait any longer. We're in an emergency – the slow burning and long-lasting kind – and now we have to respond with real transformation.

We're in an emergency – the slow burning and long-lasting kind – and now we have to respond with real transformation.

By focusing on it right here and now, and making our responses both urgent and all-encompassing, we will be resetting our world – how we live day to day, our economic systems, our energy solutions, our politics, our consumption, and our relationship with Mother Earth and each other.

By acting now, we can be well on our way to a better future by 2030. I asked Professor Lesley Hughes for her vision for the world beyond 2030, assuming we are taking the measures needed now:

Our children will experience clean air. We won't have polluted cities because we'll all be driving electric vehicles. Our cities will be quieter too. We will also have more autonomous cars, so we will dial up our transport rather than owning individual cars. We will have moved from a 'buying stuff' economy to a 'buying experiences and service' economy. There will either be a lot less flying, or else flying in bio-fuelled aeroplanes.

The big house with a four-car garage will be a thing of the past. We'll be more content with having just enough to be healthy and comfortable, rather than continually consuming things we don't need. We will value quality experiences over stuff.

Our world already has many of the technologies we need to act decisively on the climate, including a clear path to 100 per cent renewable energy by as early 2030 in well-resourced countries like Australia.

If we get this right, we'll have massive wind towers on land and offshore in the sea; solar panels everywhere, from our rooftops to vast solar farms; 'green hydrogen' to replace fossil fuels, including for making steel and cement; widespread electricity storage options like battery systems and pumped hydro; and electric vehicles that we'll run on clean electricity generated from the sun and the wind.

The amount of sunshine that falls on our Earth in one hour is enough to power our entire planet for a year. Imagine that. We can just leave the coal in the ground, where nature put it in the first place. And we already have the financial capacity to engineer dramatic transformations like our renewable energy future, even though this wealth isn't shared equally.

What we do need to find, however, is the courage and the willpower to do it. To reset our world, by fighting for 1.5°C in

In our new world, gender equality must be a given.

this decade, and by reshaping our agenda to be sustainable in the longer-term.

Women are vital to this. In our new world, gender equality must be a given. Across community, business and government, you'll automatically expect to see equal representation across genders – because anything else would be unacceptable. We will expect to see representation for people from all walks of life: young, old, and in between; across all races and faiths; regardless of politics and ideologies; whatever your sex and sexual identification; and embracing the disadvantaged, the disabled, and the dispossessed.

Education for girls will accelerate right across the planet, because all countries will realise that when you invest in a girl's education, you really do change the world. Raising levels of broad-spectrum equality will empower us as a society, and liberate us as individuals.

Mainly, we will make better and more balanced decisions about the big challenges we face as communities, as well as for the little things day to day. Our society typically will be more tolerant and peaceful, less selfish, and it will be easier to get consensus on making the changes we still need to keep on shaping a better future.

The economy of the new world will be circular. We'll outgrow the fiction of endless economic growth, with its unchecked overconsumption, within an understanding of the planet's finite resources. Waste will be minimised and nearly everything will be reused or recycled, so the end of life for one thing becomes the start of life for another, similar to the cycles of natural ecosystems. We will think a lot more about the economy's shape and stability, and how it flows more beneficially and fairly, and a lot less about its sheer size and growth.

Measuring our national economic success by the crude metric of Gross Domestic Product, or GDP, will be a distant memory. I love how some early-mover countries have already moved on from GDP as a reliable measure of progress, such as Bhutan with its Gross National Happiness Index, which measures people's quality of life;[83] while Costa Rica has made innovation and mitigating climate change core to its mainstream national economic program.[84]

In our largely post-growth economy, success will be measured in terms of the value creation and quality-of-life improvements we achieve without harming the planet or other people.

How we save and invest our own money, and the focus and performance of our financial institutions like banks, insurance companies and superannuation/pension funds, will be critical for reaching this new world, and will remain so throughout its future. Some here-and-now good news is how this dramatic shift has already begun in earnest, with global capital now swinging strongly behind renewable energy, decarbonisation of heavy industries, and the foundations of a genuinely circular economy.

The big shifts in global investment are putting the fossil fuel era of human industrialisation, which has lasted for more than two centuries, on notice that its use-by-date is fast approaching. The International Energy Agency (IEA) in its 2021 World Energy Investment report, says renewables accounted for 70 per cent of global investment in new electricity generation, which reached a total of $US530 billion for the year.[85]

Even better, the efficiency and affordability of renewable technologies for generation – like solar and wind – continue to improve. The IEA report says:

> Thanks to rapid technology improvements and cost reductions, a dollar spent on wind and solar photovoltaic (PV) deployment today results in four times more electricity than a dollar spent on the same technologies ten years ago.

I think many people will end up being surprised by how easily some of the first big steps, like reaching and then exceeding 100 per cent renewable energy, will be achieved.

One Australian state, South Australia, is already having days where renewables contribute over 100 per cent of total electricity consumption,[86] and the Australian market operator for the power system, AEMO, is preparing for renewables to meet 100 per cent of all customer demand on some days as early as 2025[87] and potentially all of the time by 2030.

Our clean energy future will be propelled by an abundance of the cheapest and cleanest electricity the world has ever seen.[88] Australia will be a clean energy superpower, generating up to 1000 per cent of the electricity we use domestically from the sun and wind, then exporting it to countries less blessed with renewable energy potential.

Where coal ships and gas tankers once plied the sea routes, we will send clean electricity generated from our vast solar and wind farms – spread across the sunshine-rich Top End jurisdictions of Queensland, the Northern Territory and Western Australia – up to Asia via undersea power cables.

Maintaining the food and other sustenance we get from agriculture and aquaculture will be one of humanity's greatest challenges for 2030 and beyond. In the new world, much of the farming will be regenerative in one way or another, and our limited and ongoing exploitation of natural resources like forests and waterways will be overwhelmingly sustainable.

Regeneration of our natural areas and ecosystems will be funded or subsidised by governments, just as they formerly promoted clearing forests and draining wetlands. As we campaign to hold the 1.5°C line this decade and launch the world on its path to a new future vision, most consumers won't buy anything that isn't helping rather than harming.

At the start of the 21st century, we were looking at the grim prospect of inter-related crises for the climate, wars over diminishing water supplies, food production including wild fisheries in collapse and biodiversity on Earth in deep trouble. A mass extinction event[89] for natural species of plants and animals, caused by humans, is still looming. So we have to act, this time to save ourselves as well as the whales and the koalas and all species, and it will take time to build real momentum.

For our new world, our prevailing culture will need to be totally intolerant when it comes to undermining Mother Earth's ability to support life, ours and other species too. We have to love her, and respect her, and reciprocate for the way she sustains us. For this, we have an incredible opportunity to follow the wisdom and culture of First Nations peoples, connecting with Mother Earth by adopting ancient knowledge and sustainable living experience.

It's about creating a new way of living that rejects today's wasteful throwaway culture while drawing on Indigenous wisdom blended with the best of modern science, and other influences including elevating the voices of women in decision-making to foster solutions to feed the world sustainably.

Though many people will continue to eat meat, typically it will be as smaller-sized portions and less frequently than we do now. People will be more culturally respectful of our food's origins: whether that means coming from nature, residual traditional farming and aquaculture, regenerative techniques, or the many closed-loop synthetic food production processes we will industrialise to take pressure off the struggling natural environment. You can already see the growing number of plant-based meat substitutes appearing on supermarket shelves as investors pump money into new food technologies. And stopping food waste must be a given.

The sheer scale of the societal transformation we need can never be underestimated. One of the biggest challenges we face is navigating our way through a just transition, recognising how big change creates winners and losers across society. We have to care just as much for the coal-mining communities facing shutdowns as we do about the small island nations being threatened with submersion by rising sea levels.

We've already endured years of so-called 'culture wars' around climate change, which have fed off the understandable fears of real people who stand to lose not just jobs and incomes, but their whole way of life. The way through this will remain challenging, but ultimately there is no viable alternative to action and change.

In our new world, our behaviours, our belief systems and all of the human capital and societal infrastructure will be needed to keep the wheels turning in our daily lives. This human infrastructure is often overlooked, or underrated, because our politicians prefer photo ops where they can don a hardhat and hi-vis vest, and make announcements about multi-billion-dollar construction projects like power stations, pipelines and dams. But it's human power which ultimately makes things happen.

I am confident our new world, blessed with equality and equity, will stand on strong foundations. Having women as equal partners in forging this new world is not optional: without us, the world just won't get there, because this journey is guided by empathy and emotional intelligence as much as it is by physics and economics and muscle power, and we're strong in all of them.

You might ask how we'll know when we get there, to the new world? As we transform we'll need to see tangible outcomes which add up to a recovery for Mother Earth, as well as better quality of living for many more people.

Ultimately, for our new world, we need to make Earth Overshoot Day redundant. We need to strike and maintain a successful and sustainable balance between minimising our consumption, our waste and our pollution on one hand, and expanding the Earth's capacity to carry us on the other.

Call to action: Choosing and changing our future will play out over a vast canvas, but we can all play our part. We can't just imagine what a new world will look like. We have to quite deliberately set out to build it together, now. Holding at 1.5°C has to be a key step ahead in this decade. But we can't stop there, and we can't wait for others.

13
CIRCLE OF WOMEN

So here we are. Right here. Right now. We are living in the defining decade. The decade for winning on the 1.5°C threshold and starting to build our new world together.

There is no time to waste. We can't put this off until tomorrow. Climate change is the biggest existential threat facing humanity, and we have to radically change everything to fix it. We can't leave anything out. We can't pick and choose this or that solution which we want to do and ignore all the others.

If the COVID-19 pandemic has taught us anything, it's that global challenges require global solutions. Everyone has to be looked after if we are to solve this. This is climate action, economic prosperity, environmental sustainability, human rights and social justice all rolled together.

Every time we're doing something kind for somebody else, we're rewarding ourselves too. Every time we prevent greenhouse gas pollution from getting into the atmosphere, we are doing it not just for ourselves, but also for our family and loved ones and the whole of humanity and every species on Earth. There is only one atmosphere, one Earth and one humanity, and we are all in it together.

We need each other. And we absolutely need women. Women supporting women. Lifting each other up. Those of us who are in privileged positions have to roll up our sleeves and do even more to help those who aren't so well off. We all need our circles of women. Shoulder to shoulder, arm in arm, action by action, getting through this decade of transformation together.

My own resilience and optimism stand on the shoulders of the amazing women I've met through my 1 Million Women journey. They are my Circle. From First Nations peoples, to farmers and businesswomen, to community activists, to a new breed of political leaders, to young women, country leaders at the climate change frontline, and to global thought-leaders and decision-makers. From all the women I have connected with doing what they can, wherever they are, to act on climate. Women who have stepped into their agency for the first time. Women who have influenced their neighbours or their supermarket or their family and friends.

Everyone has to be looked after if we are to solve this.

There's a common thread of compassion, kindness and generosity running through all of these women. It is exhilarating to be exposed to their hope and determination and to share their energy and ideas. And it means something to me to be able to be there as support for each other through these scary and challenging times. It strengthens my core, my sense of purpose.

The importance of the circle is a theme that runs through the chapters of this book. There's Aunty Bea's Circle Work. Mary Robinson's roundtable events for women. My around-the-kitchen-table experience of creating 1 Million Women. Community networking and campaigning. The circular economy. The reciprocal loop of giving and receiving. The circularity of life. This is the transformation we must have. We must open our minds to think differently.

The women I have spoken with for my book are a circle of wisdom. And there is no better way to end this chapter, and this book, than by embracing their voices. I want to share their calls to action, their messages of hope and deep reflections, all filled with raw honesty and love for this planet and us all.

Mary Robinson – former President of Ireland, who has worked so hard and for so long to bring women to the fore on climate action, and to ensure it is done with equity and justice for all:

I think women worldwide need to realise the critical moment we're in, that we only have nine years to make a real impact on the curve to a 1.5°C world. We're not on course yet. We have to do it in these nine years because it will be far, far more difficult if we don't. In fact, scientists say it is impossible after that. So it's as urgent as that.

So every woman in every context has to step up in her family, in her community, in her sector and whatever it may be in order to give the leadership that will give a safe future for our children and grandchildren. Is there anything more important?

Hilda Heine – former President of the Marshall Islands, whose small island nation is threatened already by sea level rise:

I continue to go back to remind people about the connection between climate change and human rights, because that's really at the heart of our situation in all countries. It's easy for people who say, 'Why don't you just pick up and go somewhere else?' But we're connected to our lands and we have a right to live in our lands. Why should we allow all of this privileged living to force us from living in our own land and enjoying our own environment? That's really taking our human rights away from us. And that's just not acceptable. And people need to understand that.

Christiana Figueres – the driving force of the landmark Paris Agreement in 2015, which framed the aspiration of keeping global heating to a maximum of 1.5°C:

We are at the point where we can't give up or let up. We have to move forward, and we, as women, are the ones who can do this. With tongue in cheek, I say, honestly, it was men who created climate change and women who are going to solve it. Now that is not 100 per cent true, but it is figuratively true. And that is what I think is so exciting about 1 Million Women, right? That you really carry that torch within you.

The torch that, you know, every single one of us carries, at an individual level, at corporate level, city or town, country level, investment level, whatever. We all play different roles and we have to use all of those roles to be able to bring down our emissions ASAP.

So make a plan. Figure out what your carbon footprint is. It is entirely possible we can give up red meat. We can look at the transport that we are using. We can look at how efficient our homes and offices and schools and buildings are. We should absolutely know where our savings are invested. If they are in high carbon-intensive assets, get them out because you will lose your jacket on that one. And, of course, vote, vote, vote, vote, in any possible upcoming election. Vote for those people who understand that we have a stewardship responsibility here on this planet that we cannot shirk.

Lorena Aguilar – who's worked on the world stage for climate action and women's leadership for most of her adult life:

We need to start preparing. We cannot leave this to the ones who have failed, and the white, mainly male, leaders who have taken us here. This is what they have done. This is their leadership. Where we are is an indicator of the type of leadership.

So it's time that we invest in a new generation of leaders. Look at New Zealand, look at Jacinda Ardern, look at what she's doing and what a difference she's making. It's this different type of leadership between kindness and your heart and good direction and being strong and solid when it's needed.

We cannot run away any more from politics. But what we don't want is women copying the model that has us where we are at the moment. I mean, the best indicator of failure is where we are. We need to invest in new types of leadership, men and women, young men and women. Since we hate politicians, we run away from it, but we can't do that in this decade.

Gemma Meier – farmer from Grong Grong, in the Murray-Darling Basin, Australia's agricultural heartland, whose farm now hosts an innovative community solar farm project called Haystacks:

> It's women who need to be brave enough to take up their power. Women are up against this patriarchal system that's been established for thousands of years. So we are trying to break two systems, one is the patriarchy and one is climate change.

Tish King – Indigenous campaigner from the Torres Strait Islands:

> I am the oldest daughter in my family, and so I already have these cultural obligations. I think back to the women's rights movement, and the suffragette movement wasn't that long ago. And so I know for me, that's always at the fore. After culture, being a woman is at the forefront of responsibility because we never had those rights to speak up. We never had those rights to vote. Culturally, it's always been a patriarchal space.
>
> And so, in a time where we can, wherever we are living in this world, where we can actually speak up, it's like we have no choice. Empowering women is a part of

leaving a just and sustainable future for all. We are able to be educated. So let's educate our women. We can break the cycle of poverty. It's not that easy, but those values are shared values amongst all women.

Rebecca Huntley – social researcher and author:

The power of storytelling is critically important, and the power of lots and lots of different kinds of stories told simultaneously is really important. Hearing stories of other people's transformation from general care to genuine care, moving from concerned about climate to really alarmed and ready to act can be powerful. Especially if it's a story from someone you relate to, whose life is a lot like yours.

Anika Molesworth – farmer and author from Broken Hill in far-western New South Wales:

I would love you to find that connection to the land. To feel it. To actually reach down and touch the land; to feel her heartbeat and to know that you are part of that and you're looking after it. And it's only going to look after you if you nurture it.

Nicki Hutley – economist-at-large:

When you know you're doing this with one million other people, you don't feel that, 'I'm the only one putting my stuff in the compost or making sure my plastics go here or choosing to buy something second hand.' You're with all these other people with collective action. And it's no longer, 'my small thing doesn't make a difference.'. We're building a mountain of straws that will break the camel's back in a positive way, acting together.

Aunty Bea Ballangarry – poet, author and Aboriginal Elder of the Gumbaynggirr Nation:

If someone said, 'Aunty Bea, how do you think we can go forward and save ourselves and our world?' I would say, 'Well, let's hold a ceremony and let's then hold a Circle with as many people as we can and then keep doing that, replicate that, keep replicating until other people or other women are doing that and women can lead the way with doing what I do.' I believe that in my heart. Yes. Ngaya yaanji yidaagay Miimi Wajaarr umbala – I walk always with Mother Earth.

Professor Lesley Hughes – Distinguished Professor of Biology and leading Australian climate scientist:

To me, the measure of success in terms of the atmosphere is how many molecules of CO_2 have we prevented from being emitted. Ultimately, for the climate, that is actually the only thing that matters.

Dr Anne Poelina – Nyikina Warrwa traditional custodian of the Kimberley region:

We can teach you to feel Country. To see with your ears and hear with your eyes. This requires you as a human being to unblock your thoughts and think in a different way. First Nations people think in a circle. Time is the past, the present, the future. How we became, how we be, and how we must be. Time is not lateral. It is in a circle.

Fabian Dattner – founder of Homeward Bound:

The theory I have about women, and I can't tell you anything other than my heart tells me this is true, is we are the heart of the planet.

Caroline Pidcock – sustainability architect:

Our role as women, from all walks of life, is to embrace the challenges we face while realising the potential, so we and nature can all co-evolve and thrive together. This is the opportunity to create the exciting and regenerative future we need.

Rachel Kyte – Dean of The Fletcher School at Tufts University:

If you feel overwhelmed thinking of the climate crisis and what it means for our kids then stop right here. You are not alone, and together – one meal, one conversation, one energy bill, one flood or fire response, one harvest, one vote at a time – we can change the track we are on. We can gather speed and momentum. We can ensure we won't leave people behind. We can support and inspire each other. This book is sustenance for the work we have to do ahead of us. It is hope.

Thank you so much for sharing this journey with me. Together we can create a kinder and more compassionate world, based on fairness and equity, where all living species on Earth, on the land and in the water and the skies, coexist in a sustainable balance. A circular world, where economies flow in a loop rather than pursue the myth of endless linear growth. A world where we learn from and follow the lead of First Nations peoples, with each of us knowing and revering our Country. Where we hear Mother Earth, Aunty Bea's Miimi Wajaarr, through the soles of our feet. Where we take inspiration from Indigenous culture to unite our past, our present and our future into a more meaningful way of being. A world where we don't define ourselves as consumers of this planet, and we embrace community with common intent. Where we use our money for the good of the Earth and each other. A world where we only vote for courageous politicians who will lead on climate action or even become that person ourselves. A world where we fill ourselves with active optimism and radical hope, channelling our emotions into determination and drive. A world where we are doing all we can to prevent greenhouse gas pollution from entering the atmosphere.

I hope this book inspires you to step into your own agency and find your own path. This decade needs women. It needs you. It needs us. It needs all of humanity to do all we can, wherever we are, with whatever we have at hand. It needs us all responding with love, compassion and inclusion.

POSTSCRIPT

As the manuscript for this book was being edited in the early months of 2022, Australia's western coast baked under heatwaves and faced out-of-control bushfires, while the eastern coast experienced a series of catastrophic floods in the states of Queensland, where I was born and grew up, and New South Wales, where I've lived for over three decades.

Many of the areas affected by flooding had suffered other floods in the past few years, on the heels of the lethal and destructive bushfires of the 2019–2020 'Black Summer'. These most recent devastating floods were driven by record rainfall events, which climate scientists have been warning us about for many years: with more heat leading to more intensive extreme weather events, occurring more frequently.

This is what climate change looks like. There's a simple, widely used scientific rule of thumb that each 1°C rise in average global temperature increases the water absorption potential of the atmosphere by 7 per cent. So the hotter it gets, the more frequent and intense the downpour. You get the maths.

For a 1.5°C rise, the atmosphere can hold 10.5 per cent more water; and for a 3°C rise – which is within the range modelled by scientists for the 21st century unless we act decisively by 2030 – it would be 21 per cent. What were previously thought of as one-in-1000-year floods events, which translates in mathematical probability terms to a 0.1 per cent chance of occurring in any given year, are now being recalculated because the evidence is changing, for the worse!

Elsewhere around the world, in recent months, other regions were hit by similarly extreme weather-related events with the fingerprints of climate change all over them.

In February 2022, the UK experienced Storm Eunice, a 'red weather warning' event, which lashed the south-western English counties of Devon and Cornwall. Out-of-control Colorado wildfires on 30 December 2021 forced the evacuation of tens of thousands of people in the depths of a northern hemisphere winter, with the overnight loss of 1000 homes just a few days after Christmas.

And the Pacific Northwest floods in November 2021 affected the Canadian west coast province of British Columbia, and the neighbouring Washington State in the US. As with the Queensland and New South Wales floods, the scientists analysing the Pacific Northwest events – which happened tens of thousands of kilometres away from eastern Australia – spoke of 'atmospheric rivers' transporting vast amounts of evaporated water through tropical and subtropical zones and then dumping it on more temperate zones.

In North America, they already have a nickname for this phenomenon, the 'Pineapple Express'. In this case, it involves water vapour being sucked up into the atmosphere over warm seas north of the Hawaiian Islands, then being transported east through the sky and pouring down anywhere along the Pacific coast of North America. In Australia, meanwhile, we now talk about 'weather bombs' and 'rain bombs', using more military metaphors.

It was entirely appropriate that this latest bout of global extreme weather events coincided with two more 'Code Red'-style reports being released in the first half of 2022 by the UN's scientific Intergovernmental Panel on Climate Change, the IPCC. These additional scientific warnings followed the headline-grabbing first instalment of the

IPCC's Sixth Assessment Report in 2021, which came out ahead of the COP26 global climate summit in Glasgow in November 2021, and which features in the early chapters of this book.

The independent Climate Council in Australia, where 1 Million Women climate adviser Professor Lesley Hughes is a foundation councillor, summarised the latest IPCC report released in February 2022 this way:

Right now, inadequate global action means the Earth is heading towards catastrophic warming of over 2°C. If all countries copied Australia's dangerously weak response, we would be headed for warming in excess of 3°C – far beyond anything it is possible to adapt to. We cannot afford to delay. Governments must slash emissions this decade and rapidly transition away from burning fossil fuels.[90]

The second of the two additional IPCC reports, released in April 2022, further reinforced the imperative for 'urgent and relentless action'. This final update in the series highlighted that it's 'now or never' for decisive climate action. While still holding out a slender hope that we can stay under 1.5°C, the report also suggested that even if we do overshoot the goal, we could strive to get back to 1.5°C by the end of this century – but only if we take drastic action in this crucial decade.

The message being sent to us by Mother Earth is unambiguous. The warnings are extreme, like the weather. We have to act, right here right now, and we can't wait for laggards in governments, corporations or anywhere else. For the sake of people and the planet – our collective Country – we have to fight now to hold the 1.5°C line!

A Special Gift from Aunty Bea and her Circle

Reflecting the connectivity and generosity of her culture, Aunty Bea Ballangarry has given us, you and me, an extraordinary and authentic gift for this book. It's her life guide for us, and it opens a door and invites us into her cultural process, and her Circle.

1. CHECK-IN: Before you start your day, I invite you to do a check-in. Take a moment to stop what you are doing, slow your breathing down and become aware of where you are, your position, how you are feeling and who you are. A good practice when checking in with yourself is to hold something special, like a pebble or a shell. This object, after a while, can take you to the place where you can really think about how you are feeling right now and to speak it out and own that.

For example, when I wake in the morning, I will acknowledge myself in my skin. I look in the mirror and check in with myself. I am validating who I am, grounding myself into any situation, and honouring that I am about to step into a new day. Some days are really rough, it can feel like the sky is going to fall in. When you look in the mirror, the eyes looking back at you can give you strength, support and nourishment. The practice of checking in with oneself is suitable on your own or in a group.

2. ACKNOWLEDGEMENT: Acknowledge where you are in life and where you have come from. Acknowledge the stories that bring us to this place, you and me. You may not be comfortable with your story or mine. You can't be held accountable for your culture's history. This practice is to do with owning our different cultural background and mindset. It's what we bring to the table of the current social, political and climate crisis.

In Western culture you own land. We, the First Nations people, have a reciprocal arrangement with Country which is stronger than a piece of paper. I am born into the Gumbaynggirr Nation where I have had another group of people determine my existence through colonisation. We have endured years of atrocities, massacres and assimilation policy, and have been disenfranchised and separated from our kin. Acknowledging the First Nations story is to deal with our stained history, our Sorry Business, which includes our relationship to Miimi Wajaarr, Mother Earth, before we can cross the threshold for a 'new normal'.

Many of today's 'taking care of Country' issues come from not having a reciprocal relationship with Miimi Wajaarr. For us to come to an equal-informed conversation and walk together in a shared responsibility place, we have to acknowledge our histories, yours and mine. We were educated to your ways, come sit in 'Circle' and ceremony with us, get engaged and learn our history, our ways. We might both be out of our comfort zones and that is our shared responsibility.

Accept change. Look for Indigenous activities in your local area. Get to know my people, through reconciliation week or other multicultural events. There needs to be representation from all different cultures and a greater representation of women in positions that make decisions. To get to the 'new normal' we have to connect to Country – listen to the land, the animals, the weather, the seasons, the stories and the old ways. We have to have a common, mutual conversation and make intelligent strategies. We can do this together.

3. CEREMONY: I invite you to engage in ceremonies. My Element Ceremony is a wonderful tool used for clearing and grounding on any occasion. Start by holding a handful of soil and connecting to Earth. In a group, we would each put a handful of earth in a bowl

and mix it together symbolising our unity, our coming together.

Then, proceed to connect with the air element. In nature and on the spiritual journey the wind picks up the dust and debris and will neutralise it back into positive energy again. I invite you to close your eyes and imagine gathering up negative energy or debris and placing them in an imaginary bag. After a while, imagine pulling out the bag and emptying it up into the wind. 'Or you can imagine blowing out into a feather what no longer serves you, then blow the feather away to let it go. This, to me, means we are clear to proceed.

The next element is fire. Firing the dream is using a piece of wood that I call a dreaming stick. Holding this stick with both hands close to your heart. Close your eyes and dream into the stick all the aspirations of this particular gathering or journey that will change into a reality. Dream big and be courageous in your big dream. When you feel your piece of wood is the holder of a new way forward, I invite you to place it into the flames to be fired or imagine putting it into a fire, as if bonding dreams together, giving us a collective dream. This to me means we are purposefully and actively turning an idea into an action.

To close the ceremony, you give your ideas nourishment by telling the world: this is symbolic of celebration. I do this with the use of water – owning water as my telegraph system. By pouring some of the sacred water into a river or the ocean or a stream we hand news down into the water so that it will symbolically travel to all the shores of all other landmasses. I believe with my spirit that others will hear, and I own this to make it real to me. Another way to use the water in ritual is to scoop a cupful of the sacred water and pour it over a plant to symbolise growth, opportunity and nourishment.

4. CIRCLE WORK: Sharing stories and being heard is part of getting to know each other while developing what makes us and our community interconnected, united and resilient – this is important in discussion around our care of Miimi Wajaarr, and our problem solving.

Circle Work is a group practice of deep inner listening, self-reflection and accountability. This process is simple, non-threatening and is co-created by all who are present. While in Circle we listen to others share their story without interruption, judgement or wanting to 'fix things', only speaking for yourself and about yourself. The Circle is held in a relaxed format so people find it easy to talk and comfortable to verbalise what is troubling them or what they are celebrating. I call that speakeasy.

There is no hierarchy when sitting in Circle as we sit at the same level, none higher than the others, and it supports us to become equal participants. Circle Work can support people to move from a place of recovery to discovery, in an authentic culturally safe place. Circles heal – because we are able to talk it out of our bodies. I'd like to see Circles as a way of life at the personal and organisational level. Learn this way of connecting and working together. Come sit with me and my kin.

5. HONOUR COUNTRY: Honouring is a strategy that is important for our Miimi Wajaarr and community. At the end of your day, or the close of a Circle, the invitation is to take a moment to breathe and honour all the other people that have walked with you during the day or sat with you in Circle. Honour Country, the friendships, the food – the nourishment you have received. It's no different to saying thank you at the table after having a nice meal.

My Elder-kin, they used to say little things in language, not just yarraang, thank you. They spoke to how we can protect ourselves and each other until we see each other again. Honour yourself at the end of the day, like swaddling a baby before putting them to sleep. When you go to bed at night, go over and recap your day.

When the day is marred with difficulties, bring peace to yourself. Sometimes this is not easy.

My dad used to say: 'When you have had a rough day, put clean sheets on the bed, take a nice shower, dry yourself proper good-way. Put on your nightie and swaddle yourself in bed. And you will go into a peaceful sleep.'

6. TOTEM: Having a totem, or symbol, that guides and supports you is an honouring practice. As kids, we'd find a snake by the river and Dad would share the story that had been handed down from his mother's bloodline. He'd story that we are like the snake: when the snake grows through different stages of life, he doesn't lose his skin, he grows out of it. That's how we feel. Whenever the snake is around, you come back to this place where we are sitting, remembering this moment. Stop, look at the snake and become grounded in that moment. The snake helps us to become grounded.

For Mum, it's the kookaburra. When things get too hard, kookaburra opens her beak and laughs it off. When life gets too tough, don't sweat the small stuff. When you hear a kookaburra, stop, become grounded and laugh. Don't rush the day.

My totem is the turtle. The ocean is the totem for the Gumbaynggirr people. As children, when we were not happy or niggling with each other, my granny from my dad's bloodline would say to Dad, 'Take the kids down to the ocean and let all those squabbly bits get washed away in the outgoing tide.' Near the ocean and the turtle, I feel grounded and protected.

Knowing the stories of the totems helps us to care for Country, which is not only the earth; it is the land, sea and waterways. It's a cultural practice to learn about, accept and honour this responsibility to live side by side with the totems. It is part of our natural way of being.

Aunty Bea invites us to borrow from her life guide. For our new world, we need to find our unique piece of storytelling, and explore our own relationships with Mother Earth – we need to feel her, taste her, see her and hear her.

ENDNOTES

1 news.un.org/en/story/2021/11/1105322
2 'CSIRO study proves climate change driving Australia's 800 per cent boom in bushfires': www.smh.com.au/politics/federal/csiro-study-proves-climate-change-driving-australia-s-800-percent-boom-in-bushfires-20211126-p59cgr.html
3 'Australia: After the bushfires': en.unesco.org/courier/2021-3/australia-after-bushfires
4 public.wmo.int/en/media/press-release/2021-one-of-seven-warmest-years-record-wmo-consolidated-data-shows
5 www.un.org/en/climatechange/paris-agreement
6 public.wmo.int/en/media/press-release/2020-was-one-of-three-warmest-years-record
7 www.iea.org/reports/world-energy-outlook-2021/executive-summary
8 blog.csiro.au/ipcc-says-earth-will-reach-temperature-rise-of-about-1-5 per centE2 per cent84 per cent83-in-around-a-decade-but-limiting-any-global-warming-is-what-matters-most/
9 www.theguardian.com/environment/2021/aug/05/climate-crisis-scientists-spot-warning-signs-of-gulf-stream-collapse
10 www.abc.net.au/worldtoday/content/2006/s1776868.htm#:~:text= per cent249 per cent20trillion per cent20the per cent20cost per cent20of per cent20global per cent20warming per cent3A per cent20Stern per cent20Report,-PRINT per cent20FRIENDLY
11 The Climate Reality Project slideshow 2021
12 www.nrdc.org/stories/permafrost-everything-you-need-know
13 Murdoch Books, Sydney, 2020
14 'Solving climate change needs a new social contract': time.com/6140430/climate-change-trust/?utm_source=twitter&s=09&fbclid=IwAR2-i_QEI67ygKKOOV8i8lVzZZOTxLRmaLhefg3enLo0bsH4pfdXfoAcNUE
15 Edited extract from *The Future We Choose* by Christiana Figueres and Tom Rivett-Carnac, published by Bonnier in 2021, and republished by The Climate Council: www.climatecouncil.org.au/wp-content/uploads/2020/04/The-Future-We-Choose-Extract-Chapter-5-Stubborn-Optimism.pdf

16 in.one.un.org/un-press-release/think-equal-build-smart-innovate-for-change/

17 unfccc.int/news/5-reasons-why-climate-action-needs-women

18 'Microfinance and women: The micro-mystique': asiasociety.org/education/microfinance-and-women-micro-mystique

19 Frost & Sullivan media announcement: www.prnewswire.com/in/news-releases/global-female-income-to-reach-24-trillion-in-2020-says-frost-amp-sullivan-846488109.html

20 'Wise up to women': www.nielsen.com/us/en/insights/article/2020/wise-up-to-women/

21 www.forbes.com/sites/bridgetbrennan/2020/02/10/how-womens-economic-power-is-reshaping-the-consumer-market/?sh=c75829beb4af

22 w4c.org

23 w4c.org/sites/default/files/2019-02/W4C_REPORT_Gender%20Inclusive%20Climate%20Action%20in%20Cities_BD.pdf

24 www.un.org/sustainabledevelopment/development-agenda/

25 w4c.org/full-study/women4climate-report-gender-inclusive-climate-action-cities

26 w4c.org/full-study/women4climate-report-gender-inclusive-climate-action-cities

27 'Women … in the shadow of climate change': www.un.org/en/chronicle/article/womenin-shadow-climate-change#:~:text=Women per cent20are per cent20increasingly per cent20being per cent20seen,dependent per cent20on per cent20threatened per cent20natural per cent20resources

28 unfccc.int/news/climate-change-increases-the-risk-of-violence-against-women

29 'Seen but hardly heard: Why gender parity is not equal to gender equality': www.stockholmresilience.org/research/research-news/2018-03-05-seen-but-hardly-heard.html

30 'Why diversity matters: www.mckinsey.com/business-functions/people-and-organizational-performance/our-insights/why-diversity-matters

31 www.france24.com/en/europe/20210330-pandemic-delays-gender-equality-by-a-generation-world-economic-forum

32 yaleclimateconnections.org/2019/09/countries-with-more-female-politicians-pass-more-ambitious-climate-policies-study-suggests/

33 www.unwomen.org/en/what-we-do/leadership-and-political-participation/facts-and-figures

34 www.unwomen.org/en/what-we-do/leadership-and-political-participation/facts-and-figures

35 w4c.org/full-study/women4climate-report-gender-inclusive-climate-action-cities

36 www.catalyst.org/research/women-ceos-of-the-sp-500/

37 www.nytimes.com/2019/09/20/nyregion/climate-strike-nyc.html

38 www.washingtonpost.com/science/2019/09/24/teen-girls-are-leading-climate-strikes-helping-change-face-environmentalism

39 w4c.org/who-we-are

40 'Notebooks of Foundation Challenge No 2: Gender and Climate', part of the women4climate program, page 23.

41 www.un.org/en/climatechange/youth-in-action

42 www.goodreads.com/work/quotes/10775415-merchants-of-doubt

43 theconversation.com/the-worlds-best-fire-management-system-is-in-northern-australia-and-its-led-by-indigenous-land-managers-133071

44 Pan Macmillan, Sydney, 2021

45 www.forbes.com/sites/forbescontentmarketing/2019/05/13/20-facts-and-figures-to-know-when-marketing-to-women/?sh=10ef2fd01297

46 grist.org/climate/people-didnt-used-to-be-consumers-what-happened/

47 www.theguardian.com/environment/2020/sep/21/worlds-richest-1-cause-double-co2-emissions-of-poorest-50-says-oxfam/

48 commonthreadco.com/blogs/coachs-corner/beauty-industry-cosmetics-marketing-ecommerce

49 capitalcounselor.com/beauty-industry-statistics/

50 globuc.com/news/how-plastics-waste-recycling-could-transform-the-chemical-industry/

51 'The real cost of your shopping habits', Forbes: www.forbes.com/sites/emmajohnson/2015/01/15/the-real-cost-of-your-shopping-habits/?sh per cent3D429e7de11452

52 'Why clothes are so hard to recycle', BBC, 13 July 2020: www.bbc.com/future/article/20200710-why-clothes-are-so-hard-to-recycle

53 peppermintmag.com/outfit-repeating-stigma/

54 www.bcg.com/en-au/publications/2020/managing-next-decade-women-wealth

55 www.nielsen.com/us/en/insights/article/2020/wise-up-to-women/

56 www.catalyst.org/research/buying-power/

57 w4c.org/full-study/women4climate-report-gender-inclusive-climate-action-cities

58 www.climatepsychologyalliance.org/handbook/413-agency

59 www.forbes.com/sites/civicnation/2020/03/17/civic-engagement-benefits-all-of-us-so-why-are-women-more-involved-than-men/?sh=39c03ee54f72

60 www.forbes.com/sites/davidrvetter/2021/05/26/shell-oil-verdict-could-trigger-a-wave-of-climate-litigation-against-big-polluters/?sh=103a205e1a79

61 www.theguardian.com/environment/2017/oct/02/coca-cola-increased-its-production-of-plastic-bottles-by-a-billion-last-year-say-greenpeace

62 ellenmacarthurfoundation.org/the-plastics-pact-nl

63 Our World in Data – Food Emissions Carbon Budget: ourworldindata.org/food-emissions-carbon-budget

64 Our World in Data – Environmental Impacts of Food: ourworldindata.org/environmental-impacts-of-food

65 www.theguardian.com/environment/2021/sep/13/meat-greenhouses-gases-food-production-study

66 Meat Atlas 2021: eu.boell.org/en/MeatAtlas

67 www.drive.com.au/news/norway-to-hit-100-per-cent-electric-vehicle-sales-by-next-year/

68 www.epa.gov/international-cooperation/international-efforts-wasted-food-recovery#:~:text=The%20UN%20Food%20and%20Agriculture,in%20nine%20people%20remain%20undernourished

69 updates.panda.org/driven-to-waste-report

70 www.ubs.com/global/en/wealth-management/our-approach/marketnews/access-not-permitted.html#:~:text=Globally per cent2C per cent20women's per cent20wealth per cent20has per cent20shown,USD per cent2097 per cent20trillion per cent20by per cent202024.

71 reclaimfinance.org/site/en/2022/03/30/banking-on-climate-chaos-report-2022/#:~:text=The%20report%2C%20co%2Dauthored%20by,fossil%20fuel%20banking%20to%20date

72 www.superannuation.asn.au/resources/superannuation-statistics

73 mozo.com.au/family-finances/switching-to-a-green-super-could-halve-your-carbon-footprint-say-experts

74 qz.com/1885841/us-women-will-take-control-of-an-extra-19-trillion-in-wealth/

75 www.cnbc.com/2021/12/01/gender-lens-investors-direct-their-money-to-women-led-companies.html

76 www.theguardian.com/environment/2021/dec/01/renewable-energy-has-another-record-year-of-growth-says-iea

77 cpagency.org.au/haystacks-solar-garden-updates/

78 www.abc.net.au/news/2022-02-22/how-air-conditioning-use-is-changing-in-australia/100813822
79 www.smh.com.au/environment/climate-change/sweltering-mother-from-sydney-s-west-puts-son-3-to-sleep-in-car-for-the-aircon-20220216-p59x2o.html
80 www.health.vic.gov.au/environmental-health/extreme-heat-information-for-clinicians
81 www.ted.com/talks/rachel_kyte_sustainable_cooling_that_doesn_t_warm_the_planet
82 w4c.org/full-study/women4climate-report-gender-inclusive-climate-action-cities
83 ophi.org.uk/policy/gross-national-happiness-index/
84 www.imf.org/en/News/Articles/2021/03/01/na030121-costa-ricas-president-no-growth-and-poverty-reduction-without-economic-stability
85 www.iea.org/reports/world-energy-investment-2021/executive-summary
86 www.smh.com.au/environment/climate-change/south-australia-breaks-record-running-for-a-week-on-renewable-energy-20220116-p59omi.html
87 aemo.com.au/newsroom/media-release/2021-esoo#:~:text= per centE2 per cent80 per cent9CBy per cent202025 per cent2C per cent20there per cent20will per cent20be,and per cent20affordable per cent20energy per cent20to per cent20consumers.
88 www.weforum.org/agenda/2021/07/renewables-cheapest-energy-source/
89 'Top scientists warn of "ghastly future of mass extinction" and climate disruption': www.theguardian.com/environment/2021/jan/13/top-scientists-warn-of-ghastly-future-of-mass-extinction-and-climate-disruption-aoe
90 www.climatecouncil.org.au/resources/breaking-down-latest-ipcc-report/?gclid=CjwKCAiAprGRBhBgEiwANJEY7BOiHauetwhLVnPQOJjtN1U_kjGalY2UPVgbapbiuewXEXS5nOQGrxoCCCEQAvD_BwE

RESOURCES

CALL TO ACTION

Join our 1 Million Women #1MREADY CAMPAIGN –
    our two-year campaign to engage millions more women from
    across the planet.
    enquiries@1millionwomen.com.au
Become a 1 Million Women ambassador – we need you!
    enquiries@1millionwomen.com.au
Take 1 Million Women's #1MREADY campaign to your
    school or university, your community, your workplace.
    enquiries@1millionwomen.com.au

1 Million Women

Website: www.1millionwomen.com.au
Twitter: @1millionwomen
Instagram: www.instagram.com/1millionwomen/
Facebook: www.facebook.com/1MillionWomen/
LinkedIn: www.linkedin.com/company/1-million-women
YouTube: www.youtube.com/c/1millionwomen

Natalie Isaacs

Twitter: @natisaacs
Instagram: @natalieisaacs1MW (www.instagram.com/
    natalieisaacs1mw/)
Facebook: @natalieisaacs1MWfounder
LinkedIn: linkedin.com/in/1millionwomen
Isaacs, Natalie, *Every Woman's Guide to Saving the Planet*,
    HarperCollins Publishers Australia, Sydney, 2018.

Mary Robinson
Robinson, Mary, *Climate Justice: Hope, Resilience, and the Fight for a Sustainable Future*, Bloomsbury, New York, 2018.
theelders.org/profile/mary-robinson

Hilda Heine
Twitter: Hilda C. Heine @Senator_Heine
www.councilwomenworldleaders.org/

Lesley Hughes
The Climate Council: www.climatecouncil.org.au/
Twitter: @climatecouncil
Instagram: @theclimatecouncil

Christiana Figueres
Twitter: @CFigueres
Instagram: @cfigueres
Facebook: www.facebook.com/ChristianaFigueresO
Global Optimism: www.globaloptimism.com/
Figueres, Christiana & Rivett-Carnac, Tom, *The Future We Choose*, Bonnier, London, 2020: www.globaloptimism.com/the-future-we-choose
Outrage and Optimism podcast: www.outrageandoptimism.org/
Global Optimism Instagram: @globaloptimism
Global Optimism Twitter: @GlobalOptimism
Global Optimism Facebook: @GlobalOptimism

Rebecca Huntley
Twitter: @RebeccaHuntley2
Instagram: @rjhuntley
Huntley, Rebecca, *How to Talk About Climate Change in a Way That Makes a Difference*, Murdoch Books, 2020.

Lorena Aguilar

Twitter: @LorenaAguilarCR

Aguilar Revelo, Lorena, *Gender Equality in the Midst of Climate Change: What can the region's machineries for the advancement of women do?* 2021: www.cepal.org/en/publications/47358-gender-equality-midst-climate-change-what-can-regions-machineries-advancement

Aguilar Revelo, Lorena, *Prácticas promisorias que promueven la igualdad de género y la autonomía de las mujeres en la respuesta al cambio climático en América Latina y el Caribe:* oig.cepal.org/es/documentos/practicas-promisorias-que-promueven-la-igualdad-genero-la-autonomia-mujeres-la-respuesta

Aguilar Revelo, Lorena, *Observatorio de Igualdad de Género de América Latina y el Caribe*

Aguilar, Lorena, *Guidance on Mainstreaming Gender Under the Ramsar Convention on Wetlands*, Gland, Switzerland: Secretariat of the Convention on Wetlands, 2021: genderandenvironment.org/guidance-on-mainstreaming-gender-under-the-ramsar-convention-on-wetlands/

Aguilar, L., Granat, M., & Owren, C., *Roots for the Future: The landscape and way forward on gender and climate change*, IUCN & GGCA, Washington, DC, 2015: genderandenvironment.org/roots-for-the-future/

Annette Miller

Twitter: @mimalland
Instagram: www.instagram.com/mimalland/
Facebook: www.facebook.com/strongwomenforhealthycountrynetwork/
Instagram: www.instagram.com/strongwomen_for_healthycountry/
www.mimal.org.au/Strong-Women-Healthy-Country
Strong Women for Healthy Country Forum Film: fb.watch/bLY5ZzfLjq/

Aunty Bea Ballangarry

auntybea.com.au/

'Birth of My Woman', Coffs Harbour City Printing, Coffs Harbour, 2004.

'Bea's Story' in *Changing Places: Stories of Coffs Harbour's transforming countryside*, Deakin University Press, Geelong, 2001.

'Wattle Tree Town' (Revised) in *Across Country: Stories from Aboriginal Australia*, ABC Books, Sydney, 1998.

'Womanland', *Tsunami*, August/September issue, Coffs Harbour Education Campus, Coffs Harbour, 1998.

Earth Woman, *Tsunami*, August/September issue Coffs Harbour Education Campus, Coffs Harbour, 1998.

'Our Story', *Hecate* Vol XXX1, no 1pp 146–148, University of Queensland Press, Brisbane, 1995.

'Whole Woman', *Span Issue 37*, Yorga Wangi: Postcolonialism and Feminism pp. 223–224, Murdoch University Press, Murdoch, 1993.

'I Am Here in a Centre', *Span Issue 37*, Yorga Wangi: Postcolonialism and Feminism pp. 223–224, Murdoch University Press, Murdoch, 1993.

Dr Anne Poelina

Majala: www.majala.com.au/anne-poelina

Kimberley Clean Energy: www.kimberleycleanenergy.org/

Water Justice Hub: www.waterjusticehub.org/

Martuwarra Fitzroy River: martuwarrafitzroyriver.org/

Martuwarra Fitzroy River Council, Madjulla Inc (Producers), McDuffie, M., & King, S. (Directors), *Martuwarra Fitzroy River of Life*, Madjulla Inc., Broome, 2021: vimeo. com/533047074/87705efc9e

Poelina, Anne (Producer), McDuffie, M. (Director), *A Voice for Martuwarra*, Madjulla Inc., Broome, 2021: vimeo. com/424782302

Poelina, Dr Anne, in dialogue with Nick Wrathall (facilitated by Jon Bowermaster), *Living With Nature and the Fitzroy River*, 2021: youtu.be/HcpFJG8PyQA

Poelina Anne, 'Forging the Forever Industries: How ancient wisdom can guide the transition to new economies', In *Exposure*, Australian Conservation Foundation, 10 June 2021: stories.acf.org.au/forging-the-forever-industries

Poelina, Dr Anne, Global Online Dialogue: 'Making Choices About Water', Keynote: 'Not a Water Right a Water Wrong', 16 December 2021, hosted by Civic Ledger: /water-choices. cynefinaustralia.com.au/index.html

The Rights of Nature Environmental law, Indigenous human rights, litigation, Indigenous human rights, Indigenous science and it being recognised as 'real' science, World Science Festival, Brisbane, 10 February 2022: www. worldsciencefestival.com.au/event-program/brisbane/the-rights-of-nature

Climate, Culture and Peace, 24–28 January 2022, Peace with Indigenous Peoples and with Nature: www.youtube.com/watch?v=xx4KFhkhMuc

Poelina, Anne and Hayes, Alexander, *Martuwarra, River of Life*, Martuwarra First Law Multi-Species Justice, 2021: doi. org/10.6084/m9.figshare.16601504.v1

Gemma Meier
Solar Garden: haystacks.solargarden.org.au/
Komo Energy: komoenergy.com.au/gronggrong/

Anika Molesworth
www.anikamolesworth.com/
Anika Molesworth, *Our Sunburnt Country*, Macmillan Publishers Australia, Sydney, 2021.

Farmers for Climate Action:
farmersforclimateaction.org.au/
Twitter: @AnikaMolesworth
Instagram: @anikamolesworth
Facebook: @anikamolesworthdr
YouTube: Anika Molesworth)
LinkedIn: www.linkedin.com/in/anika-molesworth-
      phd-93519187/

Tish King
Twitter: @SeedMob
Instagram: @thediaryofagreengurl
www.seedmob.org.au/
Instagram: @seedmob
Facebook: @seedmob.org.au

Nicki Hutley
nickihutleyeconomics.com.au/
Twitter: @nickihutley
LinkedIn: linkedin.com/in/nicki-hutley-b6411812

Rachel Kyte
Twitter: @rkyte365
LinkedIn: www.linkedin.com/in/rachelkyte/
Rachel Kyte, Ted Talk: 'Sustainable cooling that doesn't warm
      the planet': www.ted.com/talks/rachel_kyte_sustainable_
      cooling_that_doesn_t_warm_the_planet

Fabian Dattner
Homeward Bound: homewardboundprojects.com.au/
Twitter: @HomewardBound16
www.instagram.com/homewardboundprojects/

Emma Herd
Twitter: @emmalherd
LinkedIn: www.linkedin.com/in/emma-herd-9667204/

Caroline Pidcock
Twitter: @caropidcock
LinkedIn: linkedin.com/in/caroline-pidcock-21057a5
www.pidcock.com.au/
wayapa.com/
www.regenerat.es/
asknature.org/
www.biophilicdesign.net/
biomimicry.org/
www.regenerative-songlines.net.au/

Cathy McGowan AO
Twitter: @Indiogcathy
In conversation with Cathy McGowan, ABC: www.abc.net.au/
    radio/programs/conversations/cathy-mcgowan-indi-politics-
    federal-politics-independent/12795944

Dr Sophie Scamps
Twitter: @SophieScamps
Women for Election: wfe.org.au/
Mackellar Rising: www.mackellarrising.org.au/

Anyo Geddes
Twitter: @AnyoGeddes

C40cities
Twitter: @c40cities
Instagram: www.instagram.com/c40cities/
Facebook: @c40cities

www.c40.org/
Twitter: @Women4Climate
www.youtube.com/watch?v=GZ977RPubqc

Climate Reality
twitter.com/ClimateReality
www.instagram.com/climatereality/

Women's Climate Congress
www.womensclimatecongress.com/

Veena Sahajwalla
research.unsw.edu.au/people/scientia-professor-veena-sahajwalla
Twitter: @VeenaSahajwalla

Other resources
Shine, Dr Tara, *How to Save Your Planet One Object at a Time*,
     Simon & Schuster, London, 2020.
Adenike Oladosu: @an_ecofeminist
Vanessa Nakate: @vanessanakate1
WECAN International: @wecan_intl
Explore Byron Bay: @explore_byronbay
Saltwater Sistas: @saltwater_sistas
Brenna Quinlan: Illustrations with a purpose, @brenna_quinlan
Wendy Haynes: wendyhaynes.com/
Bushfiresurvivors4climateaction: @bushfiresurvivors4climate
Fridays for Future: @fridaysforfuture
School Strike for Climate: @schoolstrikeforclimateaction
HappyBoxesProject: @happyboxesproject
LoveFoodHateWasteNSW: www.lovefoodhatewaste.nsw.gov.au
Xiye Bastida – Mexican Chilean climate activist co-founder:
     @xiyebeara

Arunima Singh – Indian conservationist and Turtle biologist:
    @arunimasingh7
Isra Hirsi: @israhirsi
Elizabeth Wathiut – Kenyan climate activist and founder of the
    green initiative
Melati Wijsen – Indonesian Activist, co-founder of
    @bybyeplasticbags and founder of @youthtopia.world
Brianna Fruean – Samoan Climate activist and founding member
    of 350.org samoa: @biannafruean
Sisters Joan Namaggwar and Clare Nassanga: @joan.and.clare
    (younger sisters of amazing activist @vanessanakete1)
Rhiannon Mitchell – founder of Sistas and Salt: @saltwatersistas
Varshini Prakash – co founder of the sunrise movement

Better Futures Australia
@betterfuturesau
www.betterfutures.org.au/declaration_form

Zonta
Zonta International:www.zonta.org
Zonta Says NOW to gender equality and climate action:
    www.zontasaysnow.org.au.

Wedo
Twitter: @WEDO_worldwide
www.instagram.com/wedo_worldwide/

Groundswell Giving
www.instagram.com/groundswellgiving/
LinkedIn: linkin.bio/groundswellgiving

Beyond Zero Emissions Million Jobs plan
bze.org.au/research_release/million-jobs-plan/
www.instagram.com/beyond_zero_emissions/

Clare Press
www.instagram.com/mrspress/
www.thewardrobecrisis.com/podcast

Liane Shalatek
twitter.com/liane_boell

Farhana Yamin
twitter.com/farhanaclimate
www.instagram.com/farhanayamin/
www.theguardian.com/environment/ng-interactive/2021/
    oct/23/wrong-side-of-the-law-right-side-of-history-the-
    activists-arrested-in-the-name-of-the-planet

UNFCCC
unfccc.int/climate-action/un-global-climate-action-awards

MY THANKS

To everyone who has helped me on my climate journey. I am eternally grateful for your generosity, wisdom, love and support.

To my beautiful global network of women. There are so many of you and I know I can't list you all. Thank you for always being there. I especially want to thank Rachel Kyte, Liane Schalatek, Christiana Figueres, Sharon Johnson, Farhana Yamin, Dessima Williams, Robin Chase, Cameron Russell, Osprey Orielle Lake, Sandrine Dixson-Declève, Sonia Hamel, Helga Birgden, Betsy Taylor, Tara Shine, Bridget Burns, Kelly Rigg, Jan Corfee-Morlot, Maria Ivanova, Kirsty Hamilton, Isabel Cavelier Adarve, Sandra Guzmán, Irene Krarup, Amy Larkin, Achala Abeysinghe, Kathy Jetñil-Kijiner, Aira Kalela, the Momentum for Change team at the UNFCCC and so many more women.

To all those who helped me shape 1 Million Women right back at the beginning and who continue to inspire me: Wendy McCarthy, Sam Mostyn, Kim McKay, Paul Gilding, Anita Jacoby, Rosemary Lyster, Bernie Hobbs, Belinda Bean, Emily Cracknell, Katrina Rathie, Anouk Darling.

To the amazing performers, musicians and musical agents who have generously supported 1 Million Women: Melinda Schneider, Katie Noonan, Missy Higgins, Paul Kelly, Midnight

Oil, Emily Wurramurra, Alice Skye, Wendy Mathews, Deni Hines, Montaigne, Heidi Lenffer, AIM (Australian Institute of Music), Ursula Yovich, Uncle Kev Carmody, Andreas Smetena, Ken Francis.

To my 1 Million Women staff current and past. Thank you for your passion and dedication: Briana Kennedy, Caroline Boulom, Jemima Pascoe, Susie Dodds, Allison License, Grace Liley, Tessa Marano, Emily Contador-Kelsall, Shea Hogarth, Bronte Hogarth, Babs Jenkins, Holly Royce, Laura Oxley, Sarah Preeble, Bindi Donnelly, Harriet Spark, Claire Hopman, Eva Davis-Boermans, Michaella Hunt, Olivia Cook, Rhonda Lui and all of our wonderful interns and volunteers. To all the partners who have supported 1 Million Women for so many years, and who have shared our vision. A special shout out to Amanda Kane and the team from the LoveFoodHateWaste program in NSW, for helping us shape and tell the food waste story.

Thank you to all the wonderful and wise women who contributed to my book: Mary Robinson, Hilda Heine, Fabian Dattner, Tish King, Aunty Bea Ballangarry, Anne Poelina, Anika Molesworth, Caroline Pidcock, Anyo Geddes, Sophie Scamps, Cathy McGowan, Emma Herd, Gemma Meier, Lesley Hughes, Rachel Kyte, Rebecca Huntley, Nicki Hutley, Christiana Figueres, Annette Miller, Samantha Graham, Lorena Aguilar.

Big thanks to Grace Liley and Shea Hogarth for helping me to organise my brain for the chapters. To Shantelle Miller for assisting me with the interview with her mum, Annette Miller. To the wonderful Wendy Haynes for the generosity and wisdom she gave to Aunty Bea and to me for several pieces in the book. To Kim McKay for supporting me with the book launch at the beautiful Australian Museum. To my publisher HarperCollins/ ABC Books, especially to Jude McGee and Barbara McClenahan for believing in me.

To my beloved and treasured Tara Hunt, co-CEO of 1 Million Women, who we lost to cancer in 2017. To my dear friend Michelle Grosvenor who gave me the confidence to start my journey. To my girlfriends Anna Magnus and Shayne Hirsh who without fail are always by my side, filling my heart with laughter and love.

And to my family. Thank you all for your love and support while I was writing this book, and always. Every moment of every single day I do what I do for you. My beautiful children, Bronte, Jacob, Shea and Isaac; my grandchildren, Harper, Elijah and Noa; my mum, Pamela Huppert, the matriarch of the four generations. And my whole extended family.

A very special thanks to my husband, Murray Hogarth: I just don't know what to say. This book could not have happened without your love and support. You are one incredible human. (I can see those of you who know and love Murray are nodding your head in absolute agreement.)